Equality and
social policy

The International Library of Welfare and Philosophy

General Editors

Professor Noel Timms

School of Applied Social Studies,
University of Bradford

David Watson

Department of Moral Philosophy,
University of Glasgow

Equality and social policy

Albert Weale
Department of Politics
University of York

Routledge & Kegan Paul
London, Henley and Boston

First published in 1978
by Routledge & Kegan Paul Ltd
39 Store Street,
London WC1E 7DD,
Broadway House,
Newtown Road,
Henley-on-Thames,
Oxon RG9 1EN and
9 Park Street,
Boston, Mass. 02108, USA
Printed in Great Britain by
Redwood Burn Limited
Trowbridge & Esher

British Library Cataloguing in Publication Data

Weale, Albert
    Equality and social policy. – (The international
    library of welfare and philosophy).
    1. Equality   2. Social policy
    I. Title   II. Series
    301.44   HN146   77–30431

    ISBN 0–7100–8770–5
    ISBN 0–7100–8771–3 Pbk

To the Memory of my Mother

Contents

Acknowledgments   ix

Abbreviations   xi

1   Introduction   1

   1 Equality and political argument   1
   2 Social policy and political argument   4
   3 Some underlying themes   9

2   Procedural equality   11

   1 Introduction   11
   2 Equality as a defeasible concept   13
   3 Equality and consistency   19

3   Substantive equality   30

   1 Justice and equality   30
   2 The contract argument   33
   3 Equality, incentives and efficiency   40

4   Primary goods and social policy   45

   1 Distributive principles and primary goods   45
   2 Compensation and welfare   54
   3 Equality and transfers in kind   58
   4 Pensions and redistribution   61

5   Need and equality   67

   1 The concept of need   67
   2 Need and equality   69
   3 The boundaries of need claims   71
   4 Consent, risk and need   77

6 Institutions (1) 83

    1 Introduction 83
    2 Health care 84
    3 Education 90
    4 Housing 97
    5 Exemption from collectively supplied
      benefits 100

7 Institutions (2) 104

    1 General framework of social policy 104
    2 The state and social policy 108
    3 Social policy and the market 113
    4 Altruism, citizenship and social policy 118

Notes 123

Guide to further reading 134

Bibliography 138

Index 146

Acknowledgments

This book is based on work first done as a research student at Clare College, Cambridge, in the Department of Social and Political Sciences. Throughout that period I was fortunate in having Professor Dorothy Emmet as my research supervisor. She valiantly read the mass of unrelated and obscure papers that I brought to her, and commented upon them, in quite undeserved detail, with her usual critical acumen. I could not have a better guide to the dangers and delights of political philosophy.

The manuscript was written and rewritten during my tenure of the Sir James Knott Fellowship in the Department of Politics, at the University of Newcastle upon Tyne. Those who know this department will be aware of how fortunate I was in being able to work in this environment, with its mixture of argumentative rigour and cool scepticism, and I should like to thank all members of the department for their help and encouragement during my two year stay there.

I am also grateful to the following individuals who at one time or another have commented upon the ideas contained in this book: Peter Jones and Richard Tuck, for their detailed knowledge of contemporary political theory; Ken Judge, who has given me the benefit of his original thoughts on social policy and his acute political judgment; and the general editors of this series, Noel Timms and David Watson, who have not only been patient with a rather slow aspiring author, but have offered many useful suggestions on details in the text. I must thank my PhD examiners, Brian Barry and W. G. Runciman, for their original scepticism, which led me to rethink many of my earlier ideas, and saved me from a number of errors. My wife, Jane Leresche, besides restraining some of my over-enthusiastic assertions on health services, patiently put up with my continual ruminations on the subject of equality and social policy.

Finally, I should like to thank Mrs Annemarie Rule for secretarial help.

Abbreviations

DHSS	Department of Health and Social Security
EPA	Educational Priority Area
GNP	Gross National Product
IEA	Institute of Economic Affairs
ILO	International Labour Office
NHS	National Health Service
NI	National Insurance
PAS	'Proceedings of the Aristotelian Society'
RHA	Regional Health Authority
RSG	Rate Support Grant

1   Introduction

1   EQUALITY AND POLITICAL ARGUMENT

Equality has long been a source of political controversy.
Aristotle remarked that 'inequality is generally at the
bottom of internal warfare in states, for it is in their
striving for what is fair and equal that men become
divided' (Aristotle, 'Politics', V.1). Developing this
theme, he ascribes political change to the fact that
some men seek equality and others prefer inequality.
'For those who are bent on equality start a revolution
if they believe that they, having less, are yet the
equals of those who have more. And so too do those who
aim at inequality and superiority, if they think that
they, being unequal, are not getting more, but equal or
less' (ibid., V.2).
    Contemporary British politics may not display the
revolutionary fervour which Aristotle associated with
disputes about equality, but there is no doubt that the
principle is still a source of controversy. Indeed, it
has been argued (Brittan, 1968, p. 11) that equality is
now the *only* value separating the two major political
parties. Other values cut across the distinction
between left and right in British politics; differences
over equality alone serve to demarcate distinctive approaches to the management of the economy and the aims
of social policy. If this is so, one of two conclusions
follows. Either equality is too insubstantial a basis
upon which to erect major differences of political
attitude, or it is a fundamental value, in some sense,
giving rise to controversy because its rejection or
adoption has wide-ranging implications for public policy.
Brittan prefers to draw the first conclusion, suggesting
that the choice between left and right nowadays confronts
the electorate with a 'bogus dilemma'. There are,

1

however, reasons for drawing the opposite conclusion.

It is certainly true that both left and right agree on a number of consensus goals, particularly in the conduct of economic policy. All major political parties are agreed upon the aims of full employment, the containment of inflation, balance of payments equilibrium and economic growth. (1) However, there does not exist necessarily a consensus on the relative balance of priority among these four goals, and one explanation for this fact is that they are all, with the exception of full employment, the means to economic ends, not the ends themselves. (2) They are only important as methods for enlarging and sustaining the social product which is to be distributed among the population. It is a platitude to say that social welfare should be improved. Questions of political choice only arise when one asks what constitutes a welfare improvement: is it, for example, an equal distribution of the social product or a larger social product unequally distributed? If there is agreement on certain consensus economic goals, this merely shows that there is technical agreement on the preconditions for whatever social welfare improvements different people want. It does not show that people are agreed on what are desirable welfare improvements, only that they conceive these immediate goals as necessary conditions for achieving whatever else they want. Lack of consensus will arise at another level, namely over the problems of how to distribute the product of economic management. *Politically,* there is little else to disagree about.

Equality is one major distributive value. To say, therefore, that arguments about equality are too insubstantial to provide a basis for political cleavages is to ignore the specifically political elements in public policy lying behind the goals of economic management. Moreover, as Beckerman points out, to say that left and right are only divided over equality is misleading:

> It would be like complaining, at the time of the English civil war, that since men on both sides could be found with identical views on the role of the episcopacy in Scotland, land enclosures, the prerogatives of the monarch in foreign policy and so on, the two sides differed only over the trivial matter of whether the king should have his head cut off for trying to assert his power over Parliament (Beckerman, 1972, p. 32).

Disagreement over the principle is fundamental, in the sense that a decision for or against equality represents an important political choice in itself.

The significance of this choice is to be found in the connection between the concepts of equality and social justice. Contemporary political arguments about equality do not simply rest on differing reactions to the principle, with some people displaying 'pro' and others 'con' attitudes towards the ideal. They also involve disagreement as to the fairness or justice of greater equality. Those who are opposed to egalitarian policies often claim that there is a sharp distinction between considerations of fairness and considerations of equality. (3) By contrast, egalitarians assume that justice involves equality, and that greater fairness in-volves a diminution of social inequalities. Moreover, unlike the consensus goals of economic policy, the pro-motion of justice is properly regarded as an end in itself. Even if, in the short-term, egalitarians compromise on the pursuit of equality to attain other goals, this simply means that social justice is not the only valuable end in politics. It does nothing to sever the contentious iden-tification of equality with the principles of social justice. Given this fact, equality is bound to sustain political argument. There is as yet no reason to revise Aristotle's judgment that it is in their striving over equality and inequality that men become divided.

The present work examines a number of inter-connected political arguments on the subject of equality and social policy. In order to carry out the analysis I examine first the principle of equality distinguishing between what I shall call the 'procedural' and the 'substantive' versions of the principle. Although only a relatively weak political principle, procedural equality does have some implications for equity arguments in social policy which I discuss in some detail. Substantive equality, I shall argue, constitutes a principle of distributive justice with respect to economic welfare, if distributive justice is interpreted in terms of the results of a negotiation among free and rational persons over a hypothetical contract, as advocated by Rawls (1972). The benefits to be distributed under this principle include, in addition to income and wealth, provision for income in special circumstances (e.g., sickness or unemployment), health care and education, i.e., those benefits typically distributed under social policy programmes. Moreover, if we approach the problem of distributive justice in this way, an intelligible sense can be given to the principle of distribution according to need, although this sense is not the one normally claimed for the principle. Finally I aim

to show some of the distinctive institutional implications which follow from making equality an aim of social
policy. By the term 'social policy' I am referring to
specific areas of public policy, namely health and personal social services, income-maintenance programmes,
education, and, in a rather more indirect way,
housing. (4) In what follows, I shall be concerned to
argue not only that the principle of equality has
implications for the development of social policy, as is
true presumably for any distributive principle, but
also that there are an important series of conceptual
links between the pursuit of equality and social policy
provision.

2   SOCIAL POLICY AND POLITICAL ARGUMENT

To link equality and social policy may seem to amalgamate
gratuitously the controversial with the non-controversial.
Galbraith (1955, p. 77) once remarked that 'One of the
most surprising features of social welfare legislation is
its inability to sustain controversy once it has passed
into law'. If this is so, social policy does not seem to
be a good area of public policy for testing views on
equality. Why, therefore, include it in the present
discussion?
   One reason for its inclusion is simply its importance,
in volume and cost terms, for modern governments, as
shown by the amount of public expenditure it consumes.
Using the term social policy in the way I have defined
it, about one-quarter of British GNP, or about half the
total of government expenditure, is used for social
policy purposes. The public expenditure white paper for
1976 shows that in the year 1975-6, 48.7 per cent of
total public expenditure went to the five main areas of
social policy. (5) At the end of the five-year planning period, in 1979-80, the projection is that social
policy expenditure will take up 48 per cent of total
government spending. Although there will be substantial
changes made within the social policy programme, it is
striking how constant the proportion is which is taken
up by social welfare spending, even in a period when
there is an attempt deliberately to shift resources into
manufacturing investment. Moreover, this is expenditure
which there are strong demographic and social pressures
to expand. For example, as household sizes drop, with
more people living away from their parents, the pressure
on available housing increases. In addition, the pressure
of public opinion makes social policy expenditure

extremely difficult, in political terms, to cut (although at a time of rapid inflation it is easier to make *de facto* cuts by not raising expenditure in line with costs). In some areas - health, pensions and housing being the leading examples - governments, of whatever political colour, are under special pressure to raise the level of expenditure all the time. (6)

Given the financial and political importance of social policy, it seems natural that the theoretical problems of distributive justice and resource allocation should be discussed with special reference to social policy. The social services are one important method, as the size of the expenditure figures goes to show, of distributing the benefits of social co-operation within a modern, industrialised society. Not only is it important, therefore, to have empirical studies of their distributive impact, (7) it is also necessary to raise the normative question of what their distributive role ought to be.

Discussion of this problem has been inhibited partly because there is widespread belief that the social services are not properly matters of political *argument*. Many people assume that there exists a consensus about social policy so that the real question becomes the practical one of how much we can afford to spend on the social services rather than the issue of principle whether or not to spend such money and for what purposes. In terms of the differences between the political parties this view is, to some extent, correct. However, party political differences are not the sole source of political argument, and in other arenas of political debate the aims of social policy have been vigorously argued about. Thus, among people writing on the social services there is a great deal of disagreement both on how far social policy since the war has reduced inequality and how far it ought to be used to try to do so. (8) Looking at the empirical evidence, therefore, the view that social policy has not generated controversy turns out to be false. Indeed it might be argued that the degree of political consensus which exists on social policy is not due to fundamental agreement on the proper ends of the social services, but on the fact that Western economies have experienced since the war a sustained period of economic growth so that, in Klein's (1975, p. 1) words, 'social policy has been the residual beneficiary of economic progress'. Given this growth governments have been able to devote increasing resources to social policy, without cutting into consumption or investment. In a non-growth economy there would undoubtedly be sharper controversy

over the level of social expenditure, and the distribution of benefits that flow from it, if only because
general problems of resource allocation are exacerbated
in a non-growth situation. For this reason underlying
political controversies on social policy may have been
dormant for some time, but requiring only the right
economic situation to reawaken them.

Both those who have engaged in polemic concerning
social policy and those who have analysed their arguments
tend to phrase the antagonism in terms of a conflict
between collectivism and individualism. Within this
framework it is natural to identify three different
attitudes which it is possible to take up with regard to
the post-war development of the social services. The
first attitude is held by those who see the state
provision of social services as a transitory stage of
political development, which, as society becomes more
affluent, should be abandoned in favour of greater market
provision of those goods and services now provided
publicly. A second attitude is that the state does have
an obligation to provide a minimum range of social
services, serving as a safety net for the poorest members
of the community in particular, but that private supplementation of the state services should be encouraged.
Third, there is the view of those who hold that the role
of the state is to provide a full range of services, of
optimum quality, freely available for all members of the
community. These three divergent attitudes, running from
individualism through to collectivism, are then identified with attitudes to equality, with the collectivist
alternative selected as the most egalitarian solution.

One of the intentions of this study is to suggest
that it is a misconception to think about the issue of
equality in terms of a simplified choice between
collectivism and individualism. The pursuit of equality
may imply that some social welfare institutions should
have a collectivist character, but the benefits
provided in social welfare programmes are diverse. In
some policy areas market-type institutions may be compatible with the maintenance of equality. Certainly in
as much as individualists (e.g.', Friedman, 1962) have
favoured redistribution in cash rather than in kind there
may well be cases where the egalitarian should endorse
the individualist's attitude. There is in fact no
general egalitarian case for collective provision of
benefits, if by collectivism we mean state-financed and
state-run welfare institutions. Whether collective
provision is appropriate or not is something which can
only be decided on a case-by-case basis, taking into

account the circumstances of each service. Moreover, just as equality need not always imply collectivism, so collectivism need not imply equality. State-run social services may pursue many goals which are essentially unconnected with equality. For example, they may aim at maximising their outputs, in order to provide the largest benefit possible, however the value of that benefit is distributed. With distributive questions the problem of political choice is not solved simply by having collectively provided services. In some cases collective provision may be a necessary condition for the achievement of equality, but in no case will it be sufficient. Either way the relation between equality and collective social welfare provision has to be demonstrated rather than assumed.

At this point it might be argued that there is little value in looking at the problems of political choice which underlie social policy, since, in practice, ideological determinants only play a small part in shaping the size and volume of public expenditure on the social services. In the most comprehensive study to date of the determinants of social policy spending, Wilensky (1975) shows that the best predictor of the level of spending on social welfare is a country's level of economic development combined with the age-structure of its population and the age of its social security system. By contrast, there is only a weak correlation between high social welfare spending and the existence of a political ideology favouring equality. If we wish to predict the level of social policy expenditure, therefore, we should not look to a country's dominant political ideology, but to the economic and social characteristics of its population and to the history of its welfare system. Interestingly, given these facts, Wilensky also shows that the net effect of social welfare spending is egalitarian. The trend, then, towards equality is certainly present in the social services; but it is present irrespective of whether it is intended or not.

To some extent Wilensky's findings do not touch on the problems of political theory which are raised by the existence of a large social services sector in public policy. To evaluate the desirability of social policy spending does not require any particular beliefs about the social and economic origins of that spending, still less any particular beliefs about the relative balance of ideological and non-ideological forces determining the level of expenditure. However, Wilensky's findings are not irrelevant when it comes to any prescriptive role that political theory might have. Moreover, for

anyone who wants to be a 'rationalist in politics'
(Oakeshott, 1962, pp. 4-5), the place of political
principles in determining decisions is an important
matter.

The solution to this problem is to recognise that the
scope for political choice occurs at the margin of
existing expenditure rather than in relation to the whole
structure of expenditure. Certainly social and economic
factors will restrict any government's freedom of action,
so that many demands on expenditure will be outside the
political control of the government. To give an instance
of this, the American social security system, where
existing legislation pre-empts the greater part of each
year's budget, has been lumped together with other similar
programmes and the group termed 'uncontrollables' by
the Congress and President (Glennester, 1975, p. 75).
Any social welfare system inheriting past commitments is
bound to have a large number of 'uncontrollable' programmes, in this sense. This does not eliminate entirely,
however, the scope for political choice. Thus the NHS
resource-allocation formula, introduced in 1971, aimed
explicitly at reducing regional disparities in hospital
provision, making incremental changes at the margins of
expenditure, so that regional inequalities should be
ironed out over a decade rather than in a single year.
In particular, the incrementalist nature of the proposal
could be seen in the fact that the formula would finance
a more equal allocation of resources from increases in expenditure, rather than from a redistribution of existing
expenditure. A more striking example of policy choice then
came in 1975 when the 'First Interim Report of the Resource
Allocation Working Party' (DHSS, 1975) argued for change
in the 1971 formula on the grounds that with no extra
resources being allocated to the NHS the formula would
fail in its intentions of equalising hospital resource
provision. On this basis the 'Report' argued that
resource allocations ought to be *cut* in some regions to
provide the scope for improvements in others. The point
here is that this is still a marginal decision, though
no longer an incrementalist one, since the losses sustained by the richer regions would not be large in
relation to their total budgets. However, as a decision
at the margin, it leaves scope for choice. At this
level the determinants of expenditure will be political,
rather than social or economic.

I conclude, therefore, that the scope for examining
the problems of political theory which arise in relation
to social policy are still large enough to be of interest.
Moreover, the significant place which the social services

have in public expenditure make it important in itself
to discuss their distributive role. The link between
equality and social policy is not gratuitous: it has its
rationale in the redistributive role of social policy
expenditure itself.

3   SOME UNDERLYING THEMES

In developing the argument that follows I have tried to
deal with specific objections and difficulties as they
crop up. However, there are two themes running throughout the work which are not extensively raised at any one
point but which form a bass *motif*, so to speak, underlying its general thesis.

The first theme is that equality is to be taken as a
genuinely substantive principle, which conflicts in its
policy implications with other values like economic
efficiency, individual freedom and the maintenance of
legitimate expectations. Consequently I have tried to
say not only why I think equality is important as a
value, but also why it is important in relation to these
other ideals, and how it inter-relates with them in
particular cases. However, I do not think that it is in
general possible to set out political principles in a
hierarchy, by reference to which the priority of one
political ideal over another can be established. To take
seriously the notion that we *choose* our values implies
that the ordering of value commitments is not a pre-
ordained necessity. On the other hand, it may be possible
to set out some of the circumstances which make the choice
of one value over another more attractive. So, in chapter
3, for example, when discussing the conflict between
equality and economic efficiency, I have suggested that
the choice of equality becomes more attractive as an
economy develops and there is less need of incentives to
encourage growth. However, I am aware that it is difficult to select a point at which the economy has developed
far enough to risk the abandoning of incentives or a
possible end to growth. This is an area where value
choices will diverge quite considerably because people
will disagree about the point when equality becomes more
important than the raising of minimum standards.

The second theme running through the work concerns
the charge of paternalism which is frequently brought
against the proponents of equality. For instance, it is
often argued that in making redistributive transfers
after market exchanges have taken place the egalitarian
is essentially paternalist, since he is interfering with

the results of free choices made by individuals. On the
whole I have aimed to give an account of equality which
circumvents the charge of paternalism. In particular,
if paternalism is strictly defined as person A making B
do something which B does not want to do, but which A
believes to be in B's interest, then I think it is
possible to give a complete account of equality and avoid
the charge of paternalism. The reason for giving a
non-paternalistic account of equality is that paternalism
seems incompatible with the equal respect owed to all men
as autonomous, deliberating agents. There may be
occasions when the value of maintaining this respect, so
preserving the freedom of the individual, may be
legitimately over-ridden out of concern for the person's
welfare. Occasional bouts of paternalism, however, do
not imply acceptance of a general principle which licenses
paternalistic interference. If it is possible to provide
the rationale for equality outside a paternalistic
framework, this seems a preferable course of action.
Although this problem is nowhere discussed as a whole,
I have touched on some of the problems in chapter 4.2.
where I define the limits of compensation in relation to
the principle of equal welfare.

   Having set out the preliminary reasons for
analysing the relationship between equality and social
policy, I now turn to a logical examination of the
principle itself.

2　Procedural equality

In this chapter I define one version of the principle
of equality, and discuss its justification in terms of
some weak rationality or consistency conditions on
political argument.

The version of equality which I shall be discussing
is often called 'formal' or 'procedural' equality. It
is expressed in the following double-barrelled principle:
  (a) Good reason has to be shown for treating one
       person or group of persons differently from any
       other person or group of persons. In the
       absence of such a reason all persons or groups
       of persons should be treated similarly.
  (b) Like cases are to be treated as like, and
       unlike cases as unlike. (1)
The terms 'formal' and 'procedural' are suggestive of the
principle being concerned with the way in which we go
about making political decisions, rather than the
specific content of those decisions. Equality in this
sense will be applicable to the use of any political
principle, irrespective of the distribution of benefits
it stipulates. To rest a recommendation for equal treatment on procedural grounds then will not be to claim
anything about persons themselves; rather it will be to
place limits on the manner in which we settle distributive
claims between persons.

The two component parts of procedural equality stipulate two separate conditions that have to be met by any
distributive principle. Thus like cases might be
treated as like without there being good reason to
justify the treatment. A tax which was payable by *all*
red-headed people, and them alone, would not fulfil the
procedural condition of equality as I have specified it

in its double-barrelled form, unless it could also be
shown why these people alone should pay the tax. Some
reason would have to be given why red-headedness singled
people out for special treatment in this way. Again
take the converse case. A benefit might be paid with
good reason to some people in a certain category without it being paid to all people similarly placed. That
someone is old might be a good reason for supplementing
his income; but unless all similarly placed old people
had their income supplemented to a similar extent the
condition of formal equality would not have been
satisfied in both its respects.

There are, however, some ways in which the two
component parts of the principle belong more closely
together than those two examples suggest. To offer
good reason for special treatment might be thought
equivalent to the claim that one person or group of
persons was unlike the rest of a given population in a
relevant respect. To have good reason for treating one
group in a special way would therefore involve saying
why it should not be treated the same as anybody else.
Once a sub-group has been designated for special treatment by this means, it could then itself be treated as a
new reference group for judging whether all its members
were being treated similarly. In other words, the good
reason would in effect constitute showing how one group
was, in its peculiar characteristics, *unlike* the rest
of a given population in some relevant respect. The
claim for similarity of treatment would then apply
internally to each individual member of the group. The
two component parts of the principle would then vary not
in meaning, but in whether the grounds of similarity were
being distinguished with respect to a particular group
and the rest of a given population, or just between the
members of a previously-designated group.

The difficulty with making the conditions equivalent
procedural recommendations in this way, and merely
varying by the above type of iterative procedure the
domains of their application, is that it confuses the
demand that differential treatment be justified with the
claim that if differential treatment is justified it
ought to apply to all those who fall within the relevant
category of differentiation. Even if part (b) of the
principle were equivalent to taking the whole of a
population as a single reference group, so that in the
absence of some differentiating feature no one was to
be specially treated, the two parts of the principle
could not be assimilated. For that would involve an
identification between the process by which differences

were established and the separate process by which similarities were made the ground for equal treatment. Such
an identification collapses together two different types
of political argument, which it is important to
distinguish. To bring out further specific differences
and features of the two parts of the principle, it is
necessary to examine them individually. I do this for
part (a) in the next section, analysing it as a defeasible
principle.

2   EQUALITY AS A DEFEASIBLE CONCEPT

(i) The notion of defeasibility

In the first part of this section I set out the conditions
for a principle being defeasible, and suggest that part
(a) of the principle of procedural equality is defeasible
in the required sense. (2)
    The notion of defeasibility was applied by Hart (1951)
to describe the way in which at law the ascription of
responsibility and rights could be challenged in any
particular instance. There are a number of interesting
points in his treatment of the subject which deserve
notice in the present context. (3) In the first place,
Hart argues that the use of certain legal concepts, for
example that of a contract, cannot simply be defined by
offering verbal equivalences. The meaning of these terms
is too intimately bound up with their institutional
context, namely that of precedent, to allow for that sort
of definition. However, understanding the meaning of
such legal terms is not even guaranteed once the precedents have been learnt. There are pleas entered in
mitigation of a judgment to the effect that a particular
case comes under the heading of an exception. For example,
a state of affairs will be described as contractual,
unless it can be shown that there was coercion by one
of the parties on the other, or unless it can be shown
that deception took place. In these circumstances the
pleas will abrogate previous contractual obligations
because it has been shown in the particular case that
the matter is not one which comes under the heading of
a contract, and so is not to be dealt with according to
contractual precedents.
    Legal concepts of this sort are therefore defeasible.
Their use stands until contingencies appear which make
them inapplicable. A further point of interest concerns
the way in which their use is governed. Their undefeated
use is not simply given by a contrary, positive statement

of the conditions necessary for their application. So, for example, absence of coercion in contractual relationships is not rendered by the necessary condition of free consent. In these cases, the practice of the law places the onus on the possibility in a particular situation of there being no consent. The ascription of responsibilities and rights is, therefore, defeasible in this sense. The assumption is made that they hold, unless good reason can be shown to the contrary.

The ascription of equality among persons has a procedural use which is defeasible in this way. The claim that people are to be treated as equals unless good reason can be shown to the contrary does not require an assumption that people are entitled to equal levels of benefit, or even that they are equal in any descriptive sense. Just as at law the ascription of contractual rights and obligations does not rest on positive evidence of free consent, so the use of procedural equality does not rest on a belief in any substantive human equality, either moral or descriptive. Strictly the claim is not one about persons, but about the way in which we can best make distributive judgments between persons. Moreover, as Hart points out, we must distinguish between ascriptive claims and descriptive ones. The ascription of equality is not to be identified with a description of persons as being equal in any respects. Ascription is a distinctive speech-act, with its own force and purpose. To assimilate it to description of what is the case therefore is to confuse the use of a non-descriptive utterance with the factual circumstances or conditions which support or are good reasons for the ascription (cf. Hart, 1951, p.161).

To make equality defeasible in this way is, in effect, to suggest that any distributive political judgment should begin by taking all humanity as a single reference group when deciding upon treatment. Initially when deciding a person's entitlement to benefit, it should be assumed that he should be treated equally. Therefore any special claims to treat particular persons differently, by imposing either extra burdens or benefits, will require showing why they are to be treated as exceptions within the general class of men.

(ii) Defeasibility, trade-offs and the burden of proof

The view that for formal, logical reasons we must make the assumption of equality is often regarded as placing the 'burden of proof' on the proponent of inequality to

justify his position. (For example this view is
offered by Bedau, 1967, p. 19; Berlin, 1956, p. 304 and
Graham, 1965, among others.) In this part of the section
I attempt to show that this view purchases the rhetorical
flourish of egalitarianism at the expense of the positive
principle of equality. This is because in supporting
the claim the substantive principle has to be reduced
to its procedural counterpart.

Where there are two substantive principles whose
application requires conflicting treatment, it is
always possible to trade-off the value of one principle
against the other (on this v. Barry, 1965, pp. 5-8).
Thus, suppose that the principles of justice and the
public interest conflict. It is necessary that in
adopting one principle the value of the other principle
has to be sacrificed to the degree to which the alternative principle is adopted. It would be possible, for
example, to have a procedural rule in one's moral system
to the effect that if justice and the public interest
conflict, justice should always be preferred to the
public interest (or vice versa). But if this rule is
adopted, then on any given occasion on which the
principles do conflict the value of the one is lost in
proportion to the degree to which the other is adopted.
For example, the principles of justice entail that no
person be imprisoned without trial, but the public
interest may require internment as the only method of
maintaining public security. To adopt a policy in line
with one or other principle involves losing the benefits
either of preserving individual rights or of maintaining public security.

If the principle of equality is understood as a
defeasible concept, as I have argued it should be, then
no trade-off is possible between the value of equality
and the principle which constitutes the 'good reason'
defeating its application. For all procedural equality
merely states is a way of applying or not applying a
rule under particular circumstances. When the appropriate circumstances occur the equality rule is abandoned
in favour of another rule, whether it be distribution
according to merit, ability, effort, contribution to the
common good or whatever other principle is chosen. In
such a case there is no trade-off between equality and
the alternative value: any 'good reason'is sufficient
to defeat the application of the equal-treatment rule.
For all the procedural rule states is that equal treatment
should be given until reason is found for abandoning it;
once reason is found then the principle of equality must
be placed to one side. To do otherwise would simply be

to break the procedural rule, or hold to it in an
incoherent or self-contradictory form. On the other
hand, in a conflict between justice and the public
interest neither principle has built into it the
specification that it must give way to any other principle.
Though there might be good reason for favouring justice,
there is nothing self-contradictory in opting for the
policy in the public interest. In other words, trading-
off the benefits of one principle for the benefits of
another.

There is, however, a strong feeling that the
procedural form of equality imposes a burden of proof
upon the proponents of inequality. Berlin (1956, p. 305)
writes for example:

> If I have a cake and there are ten persons among
> whom I wish to divide it, then if I give exactly
> one tenth to each, this will not, at any rate
> automatically, call for justification; whereas
> if I depart from this principle of equal division
> I am expected to produce a special reason.

This connects up with Berlin's other belief that it is
'"natural" - self-evidently right and just' (ibid.,
p. 304) to treat people equally. Why should this feeling
persist if there is not a 'burden of proof' implied by
the presumption of procedural equality?

One answer is that the issue is normally discussed
in terms of simplified examples where treating people as
equals in fact results in equality of condition. In a
ten-person society in which the only good to be divided
is a cake, equal treatment of all persons will require
them all to have the same-sized share. Following Emmet
(1969, p. 124) I shall call this the view of equality as
'clean-sheet non-arbitrariness'. (4) Starting with a
clean sheet in our ten-person society and acting under a
principle of non-arbitrariness equality of distribution
will result. Hence it seems that the procedural
specification of non-arbitrariness will result in an
equal distribution, as long as no other principle of
distribution is introduced.

But what about those circumstances in which there is
no clean sheet? Here the principle of non-arbitrariness
may not result in an equal distribution, even though we
employ no other principle besides the formal one of
making no arbitrary distinctions. Suppose the ten men
were given a history in which they are allowed to acquire
unequal assets, leaving some of them rich and the others
poor. To give them each the same sized slice of cake
may be treating them equally, but it is not contributing,
except marginally and accidentally, to equality of

condition. Where there is no clean-sheet in the social
set-up there is *ipso facto* a need to distinguish between
the formal principle of equality of treatment and the
substantive principle that everyone should share equal
levels of benefit, net of the treatment they receive
(cf. Mortimore, 1968, p. 225).

This distinction can be brought about by noticing that
the principle of equality of benefit may well be the good
reason which defeats the assumption of equality of
treatment. Suppose that we start with a non-clean-sheet
situation in which ten men have unequal assets. If the
cake to be divided is regarded as income, then the
substantive principle of equality may dictate *inequality*
of treatment, with the poor men having more of the cake
than the rich ones. The resulting situation from this
treatment will then be more closely approximate to a
condition under the principle of equality than would
have been the case if the rule of equal treatment had
been followed. The difficulty with the theory of equality
as clean-sheet non-arbitrariness is that it turns a
special, deviant case of the relationship between equality
of treatment and equality of condition into a paradigm
of that relationship. It is much more normal to have a
situation where equality of condition will require
differential treatment.

This point disposes of an objection which is sometimes made against the idea of equality when applied as
a rule of taxation (v. Benn and Peters, 1959, p. 108).
Given unequal income, it is argued, the principle of
equality should lead to treating all cases similarly,
unless good reason is shown to the contrary. This would
therefore involve either a flat-rate poll-tax or a
standard flat-rate percentage tax. This imposes
obligations on the poor which they should not be expected
to bear, the argument continues, and so we should abandon
the principle of equality for another principle, like that
of 'from each according to his ability to pay' (ibid.,
p. 108). Since this does not appear to be a principle
of equality it is then concluded that our being disposed
to abandon the principle so easily indicates that it has
very little of value in it, as a substantive political
principle. This argument will only work, however, on
the assumption that we can analyse a substantive principle
of equality into its procedural counter-part. It
depends, that is to say, on the assumption that it is
correct to interpret the equality rule in taxation as
the principle of equal treatment. However, it should be
clear that what egalitarians have advocated is not equal
treatment *per se*, but equal post-tax benefit. This is

a clear rule of taxation which does not suffer from the
defect of treating the poor too harshly. Only by
defining equality in exclusively procedural terms is it
possible to sustain Benn and Peters' objection to the
principle of equality.

Why is there a tendency then to collapse the two
concepts together? I suspect it comes from thinking
about equality in a legal, rather than an economic,
context. (5) The principle that all men should be equal
before the law means that all men ought to be in a
position to expect equal treatment in similar circumstances, where treatment here signifies the consideration
and attention which is given to each individual case.
Equal treatment, then, is the good which is being
distributed, and to distribute it unequally is to violate
a principle of 'natural justice'. In the legal context
therefore it is necessarily unfair to treat people
unequally, by for example overriding due consideration
of their case, in a way in which it is not *necessarily*
unfair to treat people unequally in matters of taxation.
No self-evident principle of fairness is violated when a
man pays a high rate of tax because his income falls
into the surtax bracket, in a way that it would be
unfair to go through a different form of judicial process
for two men both of whom had committed offences. (6)

The second source for the burden-of-proof argument is
a substantive belief that men are being properly treated
when they are regarded initially, at least, as belonging
to the same reference group. Their sharing common
characteristics ought, on this view, to be enough to
secure them equality of treatment. Unlike the use of
equality as a defeasible concept, this second line of
defence for the burden-of-proof argument does imply a set
of beliefs of a positive sort about the characteristics
that men share. But in this use the assumption of
equality is not self-evident, nor necessarily required
by the nature of our moral reasoning. Plato and
Aristotle certainly would not have found an equal distribution natural (cf. Hart, 1961, p. 158). For what we are
disposed to regard as natural in these cases is a function
of our beliefs about the characteristics which men share,
and given a certain set of beliefs about those characteristics an equal distribution will run against what will
be thought natural. What is more, in such uses the
principle of equality ceases to be purely formal or
procedural. It becomes a substantive principle in its
own right based upon a particular set of beliefs. The
presumption of equality then ceases to derive from the
methods of our moral reasoning, but instead is a product

of an assumption about what men are.

Despite these shortcomings the first part of the procedural principle does have value in laying a condition which institutions ought to meet when giving a distributive decision (conditions which anyone ought to meet in fact when offering a moral or political judgment about distribution). Guaranteeing non-arbitrariness is important not only in the decisions of the courts but also in governmental and administrative decisions. The first part of the procedural principle is a rule to the effect that any agency responsible for distributive judgments, like governments, should state why they have made the decision they have. Once this procedural condition is satisfied, however, the dispute over the reason given will then become one of substantive moral disagreement.

The generality of this procedural requirement, and the possibility of being able to attach to it all sorts of substantive recommendations, means that it has no special logical connection with a substantive principle of equality. The logical gap can be illustrated in the following way. Suppose we say that the relevant grounds for differential treatment among men is provided by the rule that the action in question should promote the best consequences (Mortimore, 1968, p. 225). The egalitarian will argue that the best consequences are to be identified with a state of affairs in which there are equal levels of net benefit. This stipulation of best consequences is, however, a matter of political choice, and a utilitarian, for example, would identify the best consequences in terms of the maximum sum of benefits. In both cases the formal principle of equality is satisfied; but in neither case does formal equality entail a specific stipulation of the best consequences.

3 EQUALITY AND CONSISTENCY

(i) The principle of consistent treatment

The move from an initial assumption of equality to justifying greater or better provision in any one particular case has to be supported by good reasons. But are there any features of these 'good reasons' which are of interest in connection with the idea of equality? There does seem to be one such feature at least, namely the consistency requirement that once good reason has been shown for treating one case favourably (or unfavourably depending on what ultimate distribution is desired) all like cases ought to receive similar treatment.

Consistency is a fairly obvious rationality requirement of political argument. However, the interesting feature of the principle of consistent treatment is that its application produces results of normative interest.

What makes cases alike is that they share similar properties, for example, sharing the same degree of need, or two things both being socially useful. No doubt individuals can possess certain attributes which belong to them and to nobody else, so a person can, for instance, be the only red-head in the Cabinet. Generally, however, the properties which are relevant for political decision-making will be those which a given population cohort share. The procedural use of equality will, therefore, rest upon the claim that the property possessed by one person should serve as good grounds for treating other possessors of that property in a similar manner.

What seems initially strange about part (b) of the procedural requirement is that it is a formal feature of political argument which appears to carry normative implications. By virtue of the principle two similar states of affairs must be required to have the same normative value (Sen, 1970, p. 133). Consequently, from the purely factual premises that two states of affairs are similar in the relevant respects, we can infer that both have the same moral value. To determine *what* ethical value one of the states of affairs has, we need only determine the ethical value of the other. Thus to show for example that X_1 should receive an extra amount of money on account of his possessing property F implies that the class $\left\{X_2, X_3, \ldots X_n\right\}$, identified by its members sharing the same properties, ought also to receive the extra. But the normative implications of the formal principle are not simply confined to its use in inferring the ethical value of alternative states of affairs, since the use of the principle is also connected to the notion of impartiality. Thus, if someone were to distribute benefits, supposedly in accordance with a particular rule of distribution, but failed deliberately to include certain persons who were eligible under the rule, this would exemplify bias or lack of impartiality.

An impartial judgment or recommendation can be identified in part, therefore, with a judgment which is consistent by reference to some pre-established rule or principle. Being partial is excluding a person from the scope of a rule or principle because of who he is; and therefore partiality can in some respects be identified with the inconsistent application of rules. Impartiality cannot wholly be identified with the consistent applica-tion of rules, since impartiality also requires that

rules themselves be framed in certain ways, i.e., without use of proper names or definite descriptions which
identify persons rather than roles. However, consistency
in the use of rules can be identified as a necessary
condition of impartiality. Although it is clearly
possible to be impartial in a series of harsh or unjust
judgments, (7) the requirement of consistency not only
imposes a strong rationality constraint on political
argument, but also a normative constraint.

One writer has denied that formal equality, meaning
consistency, is a necessary condition of impartiality in
the required sense. Bowie (1970, p. 142) gives the
following example to support his contention that this
is so:

> suppose that two men are trapped on an ice floe
> which will provide minimum subsistence for only
> one man. Suppose also that both men are equal
> in the relevant aspects. In such a situation an
> equal distribution of goods is unjust even though
> both men are equal in the relevant respects.
> To follow the E_c principle [i.e., formal equality]
> would doom them both.

The mistake embodied in this argument is a failure to
realise that impartiality governs the administration of
treatment, and not the justice of its results (otherwise
we should never be able to countenance the impartial
administration of unjust laws, for which Sidgwick's
example, note 7, is an instance). What the argument
does show is that equality of distributed goods would
be a form of twin suicide in situations of the sort
described. It does not show, however, that some other
principle of distribution could not be impartially
adopted, say by having some randomising device to decide
which of the two men should be given the goods. Such a
way of allocating the goods is compatible with treating
the two men equally, providing they both have an equal
chance of being kept alive. Breaking the rule of equal
treatment would involve loading the dice (in this case
literally). There is no inconsistency in giving both
men an equal chance on account of them both sharing
similar properties.

There is a further reason why consistency shades into
normative considerations, however. Even when consistency
is taken to mean treating like cases as like, the
definition of what are to count as like cases still
remains open. The similarity claim that X_1 and X_2 are
alike with respect to property F will not always be easy
to make (indeed much literature in social administration
is taken up with trying to bring out similarities of

this sort, cf. Titmuss, 1963, p. 47, for example).
Empirical investigation will often have to establish
likenesses. Similarity claims resemble identity claims
in this respect. For just as the truth of, 'The morning
star is the evening star' had to be empirically
established, so too some similarity claims will hang
on empirical evidence.

(ii) Equity and two examples

The procedural requirement of consistency is identical
with the principle of equity. In this section I take
two examples of social policy measures in which arguments
from equity are typically employed. On the basis of
these examples I suggest that, though equity is a
relatively weak political principle, the circumstances
in which it is used normally give it a stronger,
egalitarian force.

(a) The child endowment scheme An interesting example
of the successful application of an equity argument is
given by the recent proposals to reform the structure of
family benefits. This reform was proposed both by a
Conservative government as part of its wider proposals
for a tax credits' system, and by a Labour government in
its child endowment scheme. (8)
   The essence of the reform is to move away from the
dual system of child tax allowances and family allowances
to a single flat-rate payment for each child. The
disadvantage of the old system is mainly that the
benefits of the child tax allowance increase with income
within certain tax ranges and that many people too poor
to pay the full standard rate of tax do not receive any
benefit or only small benefits from the allowance. There
was also the further anomaly that tax allowances were
payable on the first child, but family allowances were
not. Keynes, among others, disliked the manner in which
the value of the tax allowance rose with income and
suggested its replacement by a system of flat-rate payments in 1940. (9)
   Why should family benefits not rise with income,
however, and why is there an argument, in equity, for
making flat-rate payments? After all, the most
appropriate way of looking at family benefits may be
as a way of allowing children to share in the consumption
levels of their parents, whatever those levels might be.
To say that it is inequitable that families should

receive different sized income supplements is to beg the
question as to the purpose of making the payments in the
first place. On the other hand, given that there is a
specific and agreed purpose in making the payment, then
an equity argument might validly be used as a reason for
reforming the existing system.

One way of looking at family benefits is as a subsidy
to parents to meet the economic costs of child-rearing.
These costs can be detailed (see Wynn, 1970), and cross-
national comparison shows them to be fairly standard
though varying with age. Relating child allowances
strictly to *cost* therefore would in general favour an
across-the-board, flat-rate payment varying with age to
families with children as a partial, if not full,
contribution to the economic disadvantages of having
children. (The cost criterion would allow some modifica-
tions to the flat-rate principle in certain cases, e.g.,
handicap, where costs were above the average.) Abolishing
income tax relief and replacing it by a tax-free payment
reverses the effects of the present system in which
benefit rises in direct proportion to income, and makes
the benefit roughly proportional to economic need.
What is more, a straight principle of equity based on
cost looks appropriate in this case since with children
no other criteria for determining income (e.g., talent
or ability) are really applicable. Their economic
reward cannot be related to their economic contribution,
as presumably the use of the ability criterion requires,
since children make no such contribution (cf. Barry,
1965, p.169). Given these considerations, there is an
argument for preferring family benefits based on a rule
concerning costs to a benefit structure which aims to
preserve household welfare levels between people on
similar income but with different sized families.

Given this assumption, the main effect of the reform
is to distribute the benefits of child allowances more
equitably, and in particular to direct the flow of
benefits towards low income families. There is, however,
a problem with the distribution of the *costs* of the
proposal. This was raised by Atkinson (1969, p. 140) in
detail commenting upon the specific reforms advocated
by the Child Poverty Action Group, which were based on
the flat-rate principle:

> A man with 3 children (under 11) earning £7,500 a
> year would, for example, be worse off to the
> extent of some £50 a year if their proposal were
> put into force. While this is only a small amount,
> it does raise an important issue of principle -
> is it right that the burden of helping low income

families with children should fall on rich families
with children rather than rich bachelors or
childless couples? There are, in other words,
problems of horizontal as well as vertical equity.
Moreover, as Atkinson wryly points out, we cannot
accommodate this difficulty and at the same time stick
to the proposal for abolishing tax relief for children -
for without the mechanism of child tax allowance there
is no way of imposing a differential tax burden.

This is a serious objection to the reform I have been
discussing, and one that raises some intricate problems.
What I want to do is to show that its terms are mis-
construed: it relies in fact not upon the principle of
equity, but on a slightly different value judgment. To
bring this out it should be noticed that a distinction
has to be made in the purposes behind amalgamating the
tax allowance and family allowances: is the aim to
re-allocate a pre-existing body of resources among
potential recipients? or is it to enlarge the size of
the total of transfer payments going to those with
children? In practice any reform is likely to be a
mixture of the two, since to equalise out child endowments to a realistic level will involve extra money
going to those with children. Nevertheless, in principle
the two aims are distinct, and any reform can be viewed
as particularly concerned with bringing about either one
or the other. Now the vertical equity argument has
mainly the first aim, I suggest. That is, given that
cash transfers are being made to families, considerations
of equity demand that the payments be related to the
purpose in making the payment in the first place, and that
the sums involved be consistently distributed as between
like cases. If this is how the vertical equity argument
is to be taken, it follows, by strict entailment, that
where payments from a pre-existing amount are inequitably
distributed any proposal to reform the system in a more
equitable direction will involve a loss to those who are
the greatest beneficiaries under the present system.
Nothing can be done about this, unless the total
resources devoted to family benefits are increased, and
ex hypothesi this is not being proposed. Abolition of
the child tax allowance will increase the tax liability
of surtax payers, because they begin to pay the higher
rate of tax at a lower level of their income, and
will also adversely affect some high wage and salary
earners by moving them into the surtax range from their
position as standard-rate payers. But both of these
consequences are inevitable if the intention is to make
the distribution of a given amount of income more

equitable. Of course high earners and surtax payers
would be treated inequitably if the economic costs of
raising their children were assessed at a lower rate than
the costs of other children, so that they forfeited more
than they would receive under a straight, flat-rate
system. But this is not the proposal being advocated.

This brings us to the second aim that reform of the
benefit system may have, namely altering the distribution
of income between childless couples and single persons
on the one hand, and those with children on the other.
In particular it raises the problem of whether the
childless rich should pay for the children of their more
fertile peers. The answer to this question, so far as I
can see, must be a qualified 'no'. At those levels of
income children can be regarded as a form of 'consumption'
by their parents, so that the parents do not have to be
compensated for the consumption they have foregone in
having children. A standard objection to looking at
children in this way has always been that it penalises
the child of low income recipients. However, the current
discussion is taking place on the assumption that reform
has covered the subsistence costs of children, and to
that extent children are protected against vicissitudes
in parental income. We are therefore free to adopt the
consumption attitude towards child-rearing, particularly
with respect to the children of high earners.

The example of family benefits brings out an
important feature of equity arguments, namely that their
egalitarian force depends crucially upon the substantive
distributional assumptions that are made. An equity
argument for reform which is based on the assumption
that family benefits should be related to the economic
costs of child-rearing has stronger egalitarian implications than an argument based on the assumption that
benefits should preserve household consumption levels
between members of the same income group. However, it is
significant that an equity argument can be used for
egalitarian purposes. A successful argument for reform
of the family benefit system can be developed on the
basis of equity considerations alone, once it is accepted
that family allowances should be based on a principle of
economic cost.

(b) *Housing subsidies* A similar equity problem arises
in the disbursement of housing subsidies. Taxation and
subsidy policy towards housing has a wide range of
objectives. For example, subsidies may be used to
encourage 'extra' consumption of housing above the level

that would otherwise be determined by the market, because
the government of the day thinks it socially desirable
to encourage this form of consumption. Similarly tax
relief can be used to encourage take-up of housing. (10)
Despite this range of policies a government might follow,
depending on local conditions and circumstances, the
problem of equity between different tenure groups with
respect to the prevailing pattern of subsidies still
remains.

At present in Britain there are five main ways by
which housing consumption is subsidised. They are:
(a) Tax relief given to owner occupiers for the
     interest paid on their mortgage.
(b) Direct subsidies to local authorities and
     some housing associations.
(c) The indirect aid given to private tenants in
     controlled properties.
(d) Tax relief to housing associations and on the
     profits of local authorities.
(e) Rebates on rent given to tenants in the public
     and private sector on test of means.
All these five forms of subsidy grew up at different
times with different ends in mind. Rent control for
instance was adopted in 1915 to prevent war profiteering
(Bruce, 1961, p. 246) and it was not intended as a long-
term measure. Similarly the rate of subsidy to local
authorities reflects the time at which they built most
of their housing stock rather than the amount of real
resources that they have available to spend. Consequently the structure of housing subsidies is haphazard,
and often unrelated to the true economic cost borne by
the consumer. Tax relief on mortgage interest repayments
grows larger the more expensive the house, thus giving
the greater subsidy to those with the greatest consumption
power. At the other end of the market the only subsidy
which a private tenant in an uncontrolled tenancy receives
is a rent allowance, and this is only a recent introduction. This uneven structure of subsidies explains much
of the rapid decline in the size of the privately rented
sector since 1920. (11)

As I pointed out in discussing the previous example,
problems of equity arise in an acute form when there is
only a certain amount of resources to be distributed
under a given principle. In housing this is a particular
source of difficulty for subsidy reform, since any
increase in the aggregate resources going into the
housing sector of consumption will, in the short term
at least, push up the price on average of housing as
such. (12) The effect would exactly parallel those

periods when money rapidly flows into Building Society
funds.   The consequent lending allowed by the increase in
disposable funds creates a demand-pull inflation until
either general interest rates rise again or supply and
demand are brought into equilibrium by a price rise.
This tendency for extra resources to create rising prices
places an even greater need on the emphasis of an
equitable distribution of *existing* subsidies.   For
without attempts at equity, very little can be done to
help those receiving only moderate help under present
arrangements.

As I also pointed out when discussing family benefits,
effective equity arguments often depend upon a presumption about the rule which is being applied by a particular
institution.   However, there is an alternative effect of
equity arguments which is illustrated in the housing
subsidies case.   This is where the criterion of equity
leads to a systematisation of different rules which are
operated for similar purposes.   Historically housing
subsidies grew up on a piecemeal basis as a method of
providing aid to particular housing tenure-groups.
However, once the subsidies are established, it is natural
then to look at their impact on the subsidisation of
housing as such.   If we say that what is being subsidised
is housing consumption, then equity considerations
begin to get a foothold as an argument for changing the
structure of benefits between tenure groups, and not just
within them.   From the overall point of view therefore
equity considerations can be used as an argument for
altering the structure of subsidies in favour of a more
even balance of resources between different tenure-groups.

The present structure is sometimes defended on the
grounds that it encourages owner-occupation, which is
widely regarded as a desirable end in itself.   If this
argument is used, it is an implicit admission that
subsidies are tilted in favour of mortgages, as against,
for example, tenants in the private market.   But
subsidies not only encourage owner occupation as such,
they also stimulate undesirable features of the owner
occupied market.   First, they provide an incentive for
people to buy larger accommodation than they could otherwise afford, so taking up resources which could be used
for providing less-expensive housing more generally.
Second, they discourage the use of spare space by owner-
occupiers who might otherwise let rooms in their houses,
by choking off the demand for privately rented accommodation (cf. Meade, 1972, pp. 298-302).   The successful
application of equity arguments therefore would also bring
benefits in the form of reducing the support for these

two types of inefficiency in the use of available housing
resources.

The value of the equity argument in this case is that
it does make one think about the whole rationale of
housing subsidies. It may well be that public policy
should aim at promoting owner occupation, so that tilting
the subsidy balance in favour of the mortgagee is not
strictly inequitable. But to raise the problem of
equity between different tenure groups serves to bring
such decisions into the open, and make the policy commitments explicit. One reason why equity arguments can be
put to good use in this way is the apparent openness of
the equity principle, which does not itself determine
what are to be counted as like cases. This means that
one is always free to think of cases as alike in one
respect and unlike in another. This very openness
can be useful as a way of systematising a set of policies
which have grown up historically in different ways. In
this sense equity can be put to reforming purposes.

(iii) Equity - conclusion

In both these examples applying the principle of equity
would improve the position of the less advantaged relative
to the advantaged. Some writers have been sceptical of
the value of the principle however. Barry (1965, p. 152)
suggests that it is a highly conservative principle,
and also (ibid., p. 156) that it fails to give any positive guidance on the distribution of resources. Are
these two examples special cases therefore, or do they
indicate a positive egalitarian function for the principle
of equity?

They work in an egalitarian direction because equity
arguments are normally used in a context where one social
group is being benefited relative to another. The point
of an equity argument is not so much to stress the
concept of consistency, but rather to indicate the proper
reference groups between whom consistency should be
maintained. The normal method of arguing is to say that
one group should be better treated than it is because
another group like it in relevant respects receives
better treatment. Why is there a need for such arguments?
The explanation is to be found in those situations in
which a variety of policies have been followed, all of
which have similar objectives but which affect different
groups. In this respect the housing and family allowance
examples strike me as typical. Because the various
policies stand in a complicated inter-relationship

with one another, the principle of equity is a demand for
the impact of these policies to be systematised. Of
course equity can only be used to criticise practices
carried on within an institution, but this may be no
objection to its use. In the examples which I used the
purposes of the institutions in question are taken to be
generally desirable. Equity cannot be used to question
political institutions or traditions as such, but then
that is no surprise. Much stronger principles are
needed for that task.

3 Substantive equality

1 JUSTICE AND EQUALITY

In this chapter I define a substantive principle of
equality and discuss its rationale in terms of a contractarian theory of justice. Such a principle will provide
a reason for defeating the application of procedural
equality: under it people may be treated differently, in
order to produce among them greater equality of benefit.
The principle of equality which I shall be discussing in
this chapter is, therefore, a substantive and independent
principle of the type presupposed in the application of
procedural equality but not entailed by either of its
constituent rules.

Within the theory of justice the central problem is
to determine the ethically correct division of burdens
and benefits consequent upon social co-operation. In
particular, the problem is to determine a *set of
principles,* by reference to which the justice of a
particular distribution is to be considered just. However,
before discussing the status of equality as such a
principle, supposedly constitutive of justice, it will be
useful to discuss the character of the benefits whose
distribution is being assessed. (1) I shall assume that
social benefits may be divided into three categories:
constitutional rights and liberties; social status; and
economic welfare. This division corresponds to Weber's
(1948) distinction between inequalities in the dimensions
of power, prestige and life-chances. The contractarian
argument has already been deployed in favour of equality
in the distribution of constitutional freedoms and
social status. (2) In this chapter therefore I will
concentrate upon the argument for equality in the
distribution of economic welfare. This approach presupposes that economic welfare can be intelligibly

distinguished from human welfare in general, and that
distributive principles ought to be defined over the
separate components of welfare rather than over total
welfare. That inequalities are conventionally classified in three separate dimensions is itself an argument
for defining the principles of justice in this way.
Moreover, economic welfare can be intelligibly distinguished from total welfare, if following Graaff
(1957, pp. 5-6) we define it as that portion of welfare
affected by changes in economic resources on the
assumption that other circumstances affecting welfare
remain unchanged. (3) Accepting this definition of the
benefit to be distributed, I shall argue that equality is
the principle which is most compatible with the presuppositions of the contractarian theory. The egalitarian,
then, is the person who holds that economic welfare should
in justice be equally distributed.

There are a number of reasons for placing the
rationale of the equality principle inside the theory of
justice. Justice is properly regarded as an end in
itself, and therefore a distribution which is considered
just requires no further ethical argument in its favour.
However, it cannot be assumed *a priori* that an equal
distribution of benefits is such a distribution. Other
principles have been taken to constitute the principles
of justice including the rule that the average level of
benefits be maximised (Harsanyi, 1955) and the rule that
the minimum level of benefits be maximised (Rawls, 1972,
p. 303). Why should equality be preferred to these
alternative principles? The only answer to this question
is to show that it better satisfies the intuitive requirements that we want to place on the reasoning leading
to the formulation of principles of justice. Since the
contract theory of justice aims to satisfy these intuitive
requirements, this claim amounts to showing that equality
ought to be the principle agreed upon within the contract
theory.

A second reason for linking the rationale of equality
with the theory of justice concerns the relation between
equality and social policy. It has been argued (Acton,
1971, p. 58) that the provision of social services is
desirable as a matter of public policy, but on grounds
of humanity rather than justice. The reason for this
distinction stems from the commitment by proponents of
this view to a particular account of justice. On this
account, the principles of justice do not regulate the
results of free economic exchange, but merely the
conditions under which it takes place. Exchange in
accordance with these principles may produce a

distribution of benefits which is equal, but will not
necessarily do so. Indeed, whether the distribution is
equal or not in no way matters under this theory, since
the results of economic exchange cannot themselves be
assessed from the viewpoint of justice: fair exchange
is not robbery, so that unequal property is not theft. It
follows, from this theory, that provision for social
welfare cannot be defended within the theory of justice,
since the provision of welfare benefits inevitably
involves an assessment of the distribution of welfare
consequent upon the results of free exchange. *Ex
hypothesi,* this cannot be an assessment made on grounds
of justice (since this concept only relates to the
conditions, and not the results, of economic exchange),
and the rationale for social services provision has to
be provided in terms of benevolence or humanity, rather
than justice.

If this theory of justice were correct it would
undermine any principle used to assess the distribution
of economic resources net of exchange, which was claimed
as a principle of justice. I shall not argue directly
against the above type of theory, which is labelled by
Nozick (1974, pp. 155-60) an 'entitlement' theory, as
against an 'end-state' theory which does make an
assessment of the distribution of welfare consequent
upon free exchange. Instead I shall present a version of
the contract argument which shows equality to be an
appropriate rule for assessing the results both of economic exchange and of governmental fiscal and budgetary
measures. How valid the contract approach is itself
will be a matter for independent assessment, so that
the argument presented here is properly to be understood
in the conditional: if the contract approach is correct,
then equality will be the rule constitutive of justice
in the distribution of economic welfare. The contract
approach has an intuitive appeal in that it incorporates
reasonable requirements of impartiality and generality
into the evaluation of justice. However, my main
interest will be in the principles that may be derived
from the contract theory. Having established these
principles, I then aim to show that the provision of
social service benefits may be provided with a rationale
purely in terms of justice.

The third reason for linking equality and justice
is that within the theory of justice one can provide
the necessary moral premises for adopting the principle
of equal welfare as a prescriptive recommendation. The
simple premise that persons are equal in some morally
relevant respects is insufficient to generate a

prescription of equal welfare. This is so, even if one
holds there are good reasons for saying that descriptively
speaking, persons are equal. From the fact that men are
(descriptively) equal in some respects, it does not follow
that they should share equal levels of welfare. To be
sure, that men feel pain, experience emotions, have
personal relationships which engage their affections,
have a sense of self-respect, and a capacity for enjoyment
provides a sufficient ground for saying, in some non-
trivial sense, they are equal (cf. Williams, 1962, p. 100).
Moreover, these characteristics provide reasons for saying
men are equal in a descriptive sense simply on the basis
that men share these characteristics as men and on no
other grounds, despite the arguments which have been
produced to the contrary. But this descriptive claim
to equality cannot license the prescriptive principle
that men should enjoy equal levels of welfare. Other
prescriptive theories, like utilitarianism, acknowledge
the descriptive equality of men, but they can, without
inconsistency, recommend an unequal distribution of
welfare, in accordance with the particular principles
they advance. Descriptive equality is not by itself
sufficient to enable one to select a suitable principle
from the variety that are compatible with the factual
claim. To select such a principle an explicitly ethical
argument is required, and this can be satisfactorily
provided only within the theory of justice.

2   THE CONTRACT ARGUMENT

In this section I set out the basis for the contractarian
interpretation of justice in terms of the equal welfare
principle. In the account I offer I largely follow
Rawls (1972), who has given the most complete and sophisticated version of the contract argument. However, in
the version I present, there are some differences between
the theory and Rawls's account. In particular I aim to
show that the equal welfare principle, rather than the
Rawlsian difference principle, would be agreed by the
contracting parties as constitutive of justice. I shall
assume that behind the desire to promote equal levels of
economic welfare is the ethical motive of rectifying
the morally arbitrary inequalities of natural endowment
which give rise to unequal levels of benefit. In this
section I aim to show that this motive would lead the
contracting parties to agree upon a principle of
equality, rather than the alternatives.
  For the contract theorist the principles of justice

are identified with the results of a hypothetical social
contract, in which social agents bargain with one
another about the principles to govern the terms of their
association in a future society. The contract is
hypothetical, so that it is not regarded as the
foundation for any existing society, nor is it thought
to represent any other case of contractual bargaining
(outside of artificial simulation exercises). The
parties to the contract are also to be thought of as
imaginary. The results of the negotiations are taken to
constitute the principles of distributive justice.

The bargaining takes place in an 'original position'
behind 'a veil of ignorance' (Rawls, 1972, p. 12). The
original position is merely the hypothetical bargaining
situation of the contracting parties. The veil of
ignorance is a way of representing the fact that all the
parties concerned are ignorant of their own future place
in the society whose terms of agreement they are drawing
up. However, not only are they ignorant of their own
future positions in society, they are also ignorant of
their own future tastes, values and abilities. They
could be anyone in the society, not only in the sense that
anything which could happen to anyone might happen to them,
but also in the sense that they could acquire the personal
characteristics of anyone in the society as well as their
role. The contracting parties, therefore, have to
perform an act of sympathy which extends to the case of
imagining themselves as someone else, and not simply to
imagining that they might occupy the social role of
anyone in their future society.

Given the requirement that the contracting parties
must assume that they could literally be anyone in
society, the positioning of the parties behind the veil
of ignorance represents, within the terms of the theory,
the ethical assumption that the distribution of abilities
is arbitrary from the moral point of view. Being
ignorant of their own future social role and personal
character, the parties have no incentive to prefer the
systematic satisfaction of one set of desires to any
other. Instead they will have to weigh up the possibility
of their having only those talents and abilities which
would secure them a comparatively low level of welfare.
Since the contracting parties are ignorant of the process
which will allocate them to their place in society, the
theory incorporates the ethical assumption that the
possession of abilities which allow any one individual
to enjoy a high level of benefits is from the moral
point of view a random acquisition.

However, it does not follow that equality is a natural

principle to select behind the veil of ignorance
(cf. Rawls, 1972, p. 150). It might be thought that the
positioning of the parties gave them an incentive to
chose equality, if they were to be rational, and that in
this sense equality is the principle that would be
chosen by free and rational persons. ·However, this
implication does not hold. It would only follow if the
positioning of the parties made it rational to choose
principles on an extremely risk-averse basis, and there
is no reason why this should be so. Although the parties
are choosing principles to govern the terms of their
association, it may well be rational for them as
individuals to favour a society in which the worst-off
member does slightly worse than he would do under a rule
of equality provided that some others do better than
they would do under equality. Whether it is rational
to opt for the more unequal distribution depends upon
the risks that someone is willing to bear, just as it
may be rational for someone to prefer the prospect of
being a failed novelist or successful writer as against
the calmer certainties of an accountant's or solicitor's
office. An argument for equality cannot be generated
simply by considering how it would be rational to
choose behind the veil of ignorance. Indeed I believe
that no particular principle, be it utilitarian or
egalitarian, could be preferred in the original position
simply because it was more rational to opt for one
type of social state rather than another.

Instead of basing one's selection of principles on
a rational choice strategy, therefore, an alternative is
to look at the direct ethical appeal of certain arguments
in the original position. One such argument is that if
there is a moral arbitrariness in the distribution of
abilities, then there is a similar arbitrariness in the
distribution of benefits which results from those
abilities. The appeal of the equality principle is that
it rectifies this arbitrariness by giving each person
the same weight in the sharing of the benefits of
ability. An agreement to equality in the original
position represents a determination, therefore, to
compensate for unequal natural endowments bestowed upon
people by nature. The benefits of natural abilities
are to be pooled and redistributed less unequally than
the distribution of natural abilities itself.

The reasoning involved here needs to be brought
out in some detail, since it is not clear that the
moral arbitrariness carries over from the distribution
of abilities to the distribution of benefits. Even
if it is true that the distribution of A is morally

arbitrary it does not necessarily follow that the
distribution of B, causally connected to A, is similarly
arbitrary. Suppose one person wants to give another
person some money, because the second has broad shoulders
and blond hair. Certainly these physical attributes are
arbitrarily distributed, but does it follow from this
that the person should not have the money in question?
In this case the possession of a certain A gives rise
to a particular B, without it necessarily being the
case that it is unfair for the possessor of A to have
B. In this instance the moral arbitrariness of A has
no implications about the entitlement to B.

However, in this sort of case it is not clear that
what *justifies* the acquisition B is the possession of A.
If someone gives me B because I possess a certain A,
then what justifies my keeping the B is that someone
else has freely chosen to give it to me. Although
the motive for the gift may have been my possession
of A, it does not follow that the reason for my
legitimately acquiring B is that I have A. Indeed, it
is difficult to see how my simply having any ability
could of itself be a reason for gaining some benefit.
I may gain the benefit because my having a certain
ability gives me the power to provide a service to
someone in exchange for the benefit. In this case,
however, the possession of the ability is not the reason
for the benefit: rather it is the means by which I can
persuade others to provide me with a benefit.

The point of this example can be generalised to
cover the case of all desert-based theories of justice.
It has been suggested (e.g., Lyons, 1975, p. 158) that
only weak conclusions follow from the claim that the
distribution of natural and socially acquired abilities
is arbitrary from the moral point of view. In
particular, it does not follow from the claim that no
one deserves their natural endowments, that no natural
endowments could serve as the just basis of deliberate
distributions. One need not deserve what is itself the
ground of desert. However, the mistake in this argument
is similar to the mistake in the previous example,
where natural endowments were wrongly conceived to
license the acquisition of benefits. Personal characteristics or endowments can not serve as the basis for
the acquisition of benefits in the absence of any
explicit value judgment which ranks a state of affairs
superior to all others because it distributes benefits
proportionate to the possession of some particular
natural endowment. Natural features of persons, therefore, cannot stand at the basis of desert-claims, since

one presupposes the rightness of distributing benefits
in accordance with natural endowments in making the claims.
By noting that the distribution of abilities issues from
a natural lottery, the proponent of equality hopes to
make it implausible to hold that a distribution of
benefits proportionate to the possession of personal
endowments could be morally preferable to all others.
There is nothing logically compelling in his observa-
tion, in the sense of pointing to an inconsistency in
his opponent's case, since the random distribution of
abilities is a natural fact, like any other, from
which no specific prescriptive conclusions need be
drawn. But it does seem to undermine the moral
plausibility of all desert-based theories of distribution,
including those which base the distribution of benefits
upon considerations of moral merit.

In formulating an appropriate principle of equality
there are various complications to which the contracting
parties would have to give consideration. The most
important of these is introduced when the dimension of
time is considered. If equal levels of economic
welfare are to be maintained, then it will be insufficient simply to measure the degree of economic
equality at any one time. People will want to distribute their enjoyment of welfare differently through
their lives. Having regard to this fact it will be
important, within the theory of justice, to distinguish
between accumulations of assets which arise through a
process of substituting satisfactions inter-temporally,
and accumulations of assets which are a function of a
strictly unequal distribution of resources. Simply
to say that people should enjoy equal levels of economic
welfare threatens to confuse this important distinction.
A principle which circumvents this problem would be one
in which people were to enjoy equal mean levels of
welfare averaged out over their lifetimes. At any one
time, under this principle, welfare might be distributed
unequally; but this will not matter provided the
current losers are appropriately compensated.

Although such a principle would form a possible, and
perhaps the most likely, basis for agreement, it is
not the only rule which takes into account inter-temporal
rates of welfare substitution. An alternative would be
that people should enjoy equal total levels of welfare
summed over their life-time. By this principle people
with longer lives would enjoy lower average levels
of welfare than those who lived less long, but total
welfare would be identical in both cases, since the
lower average level would be compensated by its longer

duration. Doubtless it would be practically impossible
to implement such a principle, and this might be a
decisive argument against adoption in the original
position. For those who lived longer than expected, for
example, the principle seems to require that for some
portion of their lives they ought to be assigned only
negative levels of welfare. However, despite these
difficulties the principle of equal total welfare is
not entirely without intuitive ethical appeal. Extra
payments for danger money, by which people may accept
compensation for increased risk of death suggests that
some weight is intuitively attached to the length of a
person's life, as well as the well-being he experiences
during it. (I assume that such payments do compensate
people for increased mortality risks, and not just for
the increased psychological insecurity that is aroused
by undertaking dangerous occupations.) Moreover, those
people who are known to have contracted fatal diseases
when young do seem to have a greater claim, in justice,
upon resources than those who will live a long time.
Even if the principle of equal total welfare is rejected
on grounds of impracticality, its intuitive ethical
appeal may have important implications when designing
certain social services.

A further complication in the definition of the
principle is that an equal distribution of welfare may
be achieved at many different absolute levels. Since
the contracting parties are assumed to prefer satisfying
more of their wants to less, whatever those wants are,
it follows that a just level of welfare will be the
maximum possible compatible with equality. Bringing
together this point with the qualification for time,
we can incorporate both considerations into a definition
of the principle which might run as follows: in the
distribution of economic welfare each person is entitled
to the same maximum level of welfare compatible with a
like level of welfare for anyone else, the equality to
be defined over the mean average welfare level for each
person. As the aim of such a principle is to rectify
inequalities of natural endowment, it follows that any
legitimate redistribution (cf, chapter 7.1) to bring
about such equality is also just.

In drawing this conclusion it is important to note
that the redistribution is aimed at the benefits of
abilities rather than the abilities themselves. Nozick
(1974, p. 228) complains that any end-state principle
is liable to create an artificial distinction
between a person and his abilities by assuming that the
latter can be pooled together and made generally

available. However, end-state principles in general,
and not just equality, are normally defined over
benefits rather than over abilities. To pool abilities
would do violence to individual personalities; but
the same is not true for the pooling of the benefits
which accrue to those abilities. For this reason it
is also implausible to claim, as Nozick does, that envy
underlies end-state principles. The parties to the
contract do not 'desire this man's art and that man's
scope'. Rather, by adopting equality, they bind themselves to an agreement to share the benefits and
burdens of their respective social roles and natural
endowments.

If the rationale of equality is based upon a
conviction about the pooling of the benefits of
abilities, it is reasonable to ask how basic an argument
this is, since alternative justifications of equality
may be offered within the contract framework. For
example Nagel (1973, p. 231) has argued against Rawls's
difference principle and in favour of equality on the
grounds that economic inequality is likely to undermine
peoples' sense of self-respect and self-esteem. A consistent schedule of rewards 'inevitably affects peoples'
sense of their intrinsic worth, and any society operating
on the difference principle will have a meritocratic
flavour' (ibid.). Income inequality, even when restricted
by something as egalitarian as the difference principle,
may, according to this argument, undermine self-respect.

There are two major problems with using an argument
of this sort as a defence of economic equality. First,
it misses the distinction between justified and unjustified resentment at unequal rewards, and therefore
a justified and an unjustified loss of self-respect.
If people are independently convinced that a schedule
of unequal rewards is just, then there is no reason why
they need feel any resentment or loss of self-esteem
because others are enjoying a higher level of benefits
than they are. What matters is not the brute fact of
economic inequality, but how people conceive that fact.
It may well be that if people were convinced of the
justice of the difference principle, then they would
feel no loss of self-esteem should they turn out to be
in social groups with low levels of welfare. The point
is that feelings of self-esteem are parasitic upon
conceptions of justice, and it is impossible to use the
argument from self-esteem to support an argument for
one particular principle of justice from a set of
viable options.

The second point to make on Nagel's suggestion is

that a sense of self-esteem can be included as an argument
in individual utility functions. It may well be that
individual welfare is lowered by an increase in economic
inequality because it increases resentment or envy, but
whether this leads to a net drop in individual welfare
will depend on whether or not the inequality would bring
compensating advantages. Under a Rawlsian difference
principle, for example, the compensating advantages
would be an improved standard of living. How the
advantages and disadvantages relate is essentially an
empirical question concerning peoples' utility functions.
It is possible that an increase in economic inequality
may lead to a loss of self-respect among poorer members
of the population which could not be compensated out
of increases in the standard of living. Whether it
would do so is an empirical matter that is likely to
depend upon circumstances. The present argument
should of course be kept separate from the question of
whether there are any independent grounds for treating
people with equal respect. As I have already pointed
out, the contract argument has been deployed in the
assessment of inequalities of social status, and there
are grounds for saying that people ought to be accorded
equality of respect as an end in itself. This is
altogether a separate matter, however, from the question
of whether economic equality is required as a pre-
condition for social equality. If there is an independent argument for economic equality, then it must
appeal to the ethical value of pooling the benefits of
naturally-distributed ability. This approach is more
basic than a consequentialist argument which places
value on economic equality only in so far as it promotes
self-respect.

3 EQUALITY, INCENTIVES AND EFFICIENCY

Based on a claim about the arbitrary distribution of
abilities, therefore, equality of economic welfare is
initially appealing. In the long run, however, it may
come to seem unattractive, because it incorporates only
weak demands of efficiency. In this respect it compares
unfavourably with Rawls's difference principle, under
which certain inequalities will be justified if they
work to the advantage of the least well-off. Under
Rawlsian principles, then, the worst-off person will
be better-off than he might be in an egalitarian
system. Why should equality, in these circumsatnces, be
considered a superior rule of justice when compared with

the difference principle? To answer this question I
shall consider it in connection with the example of
incentives, whose payment is allowed under the difference
principle provided they work to the advantage of the
least well-off. I aim to show that it is a mistake to
incorporate the principle of efficiency into the
definition of justice. Justice and efficiency are
separate values, and although the latter may sometimes
be preferred to the former this is in itself no reason for
amalgamating them together.

It is useful for present purposes to divide incentives
into two categories: those payments, like danger money,
which can be regarded as compensation for the loss of
welfare involved in a particular occupation or social
role; and second, those payments which are made in
exchange for a scarce skill or talent, which take the
form of rent extracted by the possessors of the talent.
The latter payments serve, by definition, to raise
a person's level of welfare above the average, whereas
the former payments do not. The first type of incentive
may be called $incentives_1$ and the second $incentives_2$.
Under the principle of equality the payment of $incentives_1$
is justified, because without it a person's economic
welfare will be lower than the average since he
performs a social task involving heavy costs to himself.
This is part of the importance of defining equality over
economic welfare, rather than some particular benefit
like income. Although, as I shall argue later (chapter
4.1), it is necessary for practical purposes to define
distributive principles over particular benefits, it is
important to realise that this does not imply that
equality should be judged exclusively in those terms,
since the welfare implications of income distribution
are what matter. Using the principle of equal welfare
as a criterion, it is clear that incentives would be
licensed under considerations of justice.

However, if in the original position the notion of
payment by desert is rejected, then the payment of
$incentives_2$ must be similarly rejected. For $incentives_2$
represent a process by which arbitrarily distributed
abilities are used to secure welfare gains by some
people, where the benefits in question could be redistributed in accordance with a rule of equality.
Indeed the only basis on which differential payments
could be justified would either be in terms of an explicit
desert argument, by which some particular talents simply
merited more than others, or in terms of an entitlement
theory of justice, by which the results of economic
exchange simply could not be assessed. However, the

presuppositions, which I have argued would be agreed
in the original position, rule out both these alternatives.
An agreement to compensate for natural disadvantages
can appeal neither to merit nor to the unordered
results of exchange, for both these latter criteria
gear the provision of benefits to some particular sets
of abilities distributed among members of the population.

The justification of incentives$_2$ can also be couched
in terms of efficiency. Some people may simply not
employ their talents unless they can extract a rental
value from their use which is greater than they could
achieve under equality. If talents and abilities are
not used for this reason, the total social product may
drop, and the minimum level of well-being reduced in
the community.

How important is the loss of efficiency implied by
a preference for equality over the difference principle?
My answer to this question is that it is important *as a
loss of efficiency*, but not as a diminution of justice.
Equality, by excluding the payment of incentives$_2$, may
be incompatible with the demands of efficiency, but the
conclusion to be drawn from this is that the values of
social justice and efficiency often conflict, and that,
when it comes to making practical economic and social
policy judgments, the one value will have to be traded-
off against the other. There is, however, no reason
why the demands of efficiency should be incorporated
into the principles of justice.

An important case where a conflict between justice
and efficiency may arise is in a poor economy, where
the bulk of the population is below a subsistence
standard of living. In such a case inequality may be
necessary as a method of developing the requisite skills
and abilities to promote economic growth. Efficiency in
this sort of case may rank higher than the pursuit of
social justice. As the level of economic development
rises, however, it becomes possible to achieve greater
justice at the expense of further growth. This process
is best described on the egalitarian account of justice
as one in which considerations of justice come to
outweigh considerations of efficiency rather than a
process under which rules of justice are consistently
employed throughout development.

This conflict between justice and efficiency is
implied by the conclusion of the parties' reasoning in
the original position. However, it is also supported
by certain moral intuitions on the subject of justice.
For example, incentives$_2$ are in general more likely to be
regarded as a means rather than an end in themselves

(cf. Sen, 1973, p. 104). To this extent they will not
be constitutive of justice, but at best a method of
attaining a required degree of prosperity on which the
institutions of a just society will rest. I do not
know how true Tawney's (1921, p. 220) dictum is that
everyone realises that when it comes to really important
things no decent man holds out for what he is worth.
But if it is at all accurate in capturing peoples' moral
intuitions, it would provide further support for
separating the principles of efficiency and justice.

There remains the problem of altruism. It may be
urged that the difference principle, or some similar
variant, is superior to equality because it demands less
altruism on the part of those who could extract rent
from scarce talents and abilities (Rawls, 1972, p. 129).
Principles of justice should take people as they are,
rather than aim to transform them into something else.

It is perhaps worth noting in this context that
equality demands less altruism than one other frequently
canvassed principle, that of utility. Equality requires
altruism, on the part of those who do well in the natural
lottery, only up to the level at which people share
equally in the benefits of social co-operation.
Determinate limits are therefore placed upon the obligations which people have to contribute towards the social
product, and it is in this respect that equality differs
from the principle of utility. As Godwin pointed out,
this latter principle does not allow people to claim
individual rights on the social product; it merely
places upon them an obligation to maximise the value
of the social product for the benefit of other people. (4)

However, this contrast between the two principles
may merely underline the fact that both equality and
utility are end-state principles requiring too much
altruism. In answer to this point with reference to
the principle of equality, it should be stressed that
the ethical arguments appropriate to the original position
issue in principles of justice, not the principles which
would correctly evaluate the right set of public policies
all things considered. For this task the principles of
social justice will have to be supplemented by further,
and sometimes conflicting, principles of efficiency,
practicality and savings or investment. Thus, in
recognising a less extensive altruism than would be
required by the principle of equality, it might be
appropriate to reward certain talents or abilities with
incentives$_2$ as a contribution to efficiency or as a
practical necessity. This is perfectly compatible with
accepting equality as a principle of justice, provided

that it is recognised that it may not always be desirable
or practical, all things considered, simply to opt for
policies based upon justice.

What scope does this interpretation of justice give
to the original idea of contract theory that society
should be viewed as though it were based upon a free
contract? Under this interpretation, it seems, society
is no longer seen as having a contractual foundation,
but the original position argument represents only a
device, like that of an 'ideal observer', for determining
what Sidgwick (1874, p. 273) called 'an ideal system of
rules of distribution which ought to exist'. And in this
respect it might seem difficult to see what distinctive-
ness contract theory has by comparison with an alternative
like ideal observer theory. The difference lies primarily
in the ethical argument to which the contract theory
gives rise. In particular, although it is not possible
to view the whole of a society as founded on a social
contract, it is necessary when studying particular
institutions to give them a contractual rationale. For
example, the inter-generational distribution of income
can be given a contractual basis (chapter 4.4) as can
certain institutional forms of health care (chapter 6.2).
In both these cases, the elements of social justice may
be seen to correspond with behaviour based upon the
assumption that benefits should be pooled. The contract
argument is not only an illuminating metaphor, representing the ethical assumption that benefits should be pooled,
it will also be seen to have distinct institutional
implications in political arguments about social policy.

4 Primary goods and social policy

Equalising welfare is an abstract aim. So, even if we accept that social justice requires each person to enjoy equal levels of welfare, we still need some method by which we can translate this principle into a practicable aim of public policy. In this chapter I examine the theory of primary goods as a means of making this translation, and I discuss some of the difficulties which arise when equalising primary goods is made an objective of public policy.

The distinction between economic welfare and primary goods is, to some extent, implicit in the distinction which was of some importance in the last chapter between personal abilities and the benefits which accrue to their possessors. However, these distinctions are not exactly symmetrical, since there are some benefits accruing to a person which either cannot or should not be redistributed to others. For example, suppose I can earn a good income through my abilities as a tennis player. Like any other end-state principle, the rule of equality requires the redistribution of this income, in this case so that it is no higher than other comparable incomes. However, income is not the only benefit which I may derive from playing tennis well. I may also obtain personal satisfaction in the exercise of my skill, and this is itself a benefit which accrues to me by virtue of the (arbitrarily distributed) ability I possess. Unlike the benefits of income, the personal satisfaction I obtain cannot be redistributed to others, not simply because there are practical difficulties of measurement and so forth, but because there is a logical impossibility in making the transfer. If a tennis player takes satisfaction in his talents, then his talents are

intensionally related to his own feelings: no one else
can take satisfaction in someone else's skills, all they
can do is admire them or take up some other outsider's
attitude.

Not all benefits therefore are available for public
redistribution, and this fact gives a clue to those
benefits which ought to be included in the list of
primary goods. Most obviously, they should include those
benefits like income and wealth which are conventionally
regarded in a society as the means to welfare improvements. Such goods ought to be included because they
standardly provide people with the means to satisfy their
wants and improve their welfare. This is rather different
from saying that they are primary goods because they
would be agreed as such in the original position. This
latter suggestion has been made (Rawls, 1972, p. 92),
and primary goods have been defined as those benefits
it would be rational to want in the original position
if one knew one was going to want anything at all. The
difficulty with this approach is that there are some
patterns of life, conforming to specific conceptions
of the good, which may not require wealth and income for
their fulfilment. Certain primary goods may not be the
appropriate benefits to distribute in all forms of
society. However, in societies in which income and
wealth are conventionally and appropriately regarded as
the means to improved welfare, it seems reasonable that
they should form the subject of distributive principles.
To put the matter this way avoids the suggestion that
the theory of primary goods biases the deliberation of
the original position in favour of a particular set of
conceptions of the good, whilst retaining what is
essential, namely that substantive benefits be included
within the scope of distributive principles.

It is also important to define distributive principles
over benefits like income and wealth, not simply because
of the logical impossibility of redistributing some
other types of benefits, but also because of the intrinsic
advantages of limiting those goods which are to be
distributed. By limiting the benefits to be redistributed
to goods like income, the amount of coercion which has
to be applied to those who do well in the natural
lottery is reduced. Correspondingly a concern for
income and wealth distribution also limits the
responsibilities which society incurs through adopting
a specific principle over the distribution of welfare.
By limiting the scope of redistribution to primary goods
society does not stifle personal initiative and
responsibility. By rectifying the inequalities of

natural endowment in the means to welfare, society does
not assume the role of *guaranteeing* each individual equal
levels of welfare. Instead bridging the gap between the
means to welfare and its attainment remains the
responsibility of the individual.

However, it is insufficient simply to specify income
and wealth as the benefits to be distributed. At least
there must be some consideration given to individual
mixes between income and leisure. If a person prefers
to spend more of his day working in order to ensure a
higher income, it would be inequitable to tax away his
subsequent economic benefits and redistribute them to
persons who prefer leisure to income. Some weight must
therefore be given to welfare considerations independent
of income. A similar situation arises over the
relationship between income and work conditions. Simply
to define distributive principles over the primary goods
of income and wealth will not enable one to distinguish
between different types of incentive as I did in the
previous chapter. Higher incomes would not be allowed
to compensate for poor or dangerous work conditions
because no attention could be given to the problems of
welfare which arise in relation to income. (1)   It is
for reasons like this, I suspect, that proponents of end-
state principles have advocated proportionate taxes on
income rather than the complete elimination of
differentials. The latter would involve as many
inequities as a system in which there was no redistribution.

Moreover, there is a further problem in restricting
the list of primary goods simply to income and wealth,
since this ignores those cases in which special
circumstances mean that people will experience lower
level of welfare on the same income as other members of
the community (cf. Barry, 1973, pp. 55-6; Dasgupta,
1974, p. 326). Variations in individual welfare
functions may mean that individuals will experience
large variations in welfare on the same income because
their circumstances require greater expenditure in order
to achieve the same level of satisfaction. An obvious
example here would be the comparison between a physically-
handicapped person and someone who is not handicapped.
The former has greater needs than the latter, if they
are to achieve the same level of well-being. (2)
Travelling costs will be greater, his house may require
special fitments to suit his circumstances, and he may
require frequent consultation with medical specialists.
Thus merely to give the two people the same income would
fail to maintain an equal level of welfare. The point

is best made in relation to physical handicap, because
the source of the variation in welfare function is most
obvious in that case. However, similar variations of
welfare function may arise for single parents, large
families or the old. In each case the importance of
variations in welfare functions undermines any simple
reliance on comparing economic welfare by looking at the
distribution of income.

It would, however, be a mistake to conclude from these
examples that the aim of basing distributive principles
on primary goods comparisons was theoretically unattractive. Indeed the harder one presses the case that
variations in individual welfare functions give rise to
special claims upon income, the less practical the
redistributive aims of any society will look. Such
detailed knowledge of individual circumstances seems
required that no one would be in a position to acquire
and process the requisite information. Moreover, public
policy makers would not only have to take into account
variations in individual circumstances, with appropriate
weights being assigned to such variables as mobility
impairment as against short-sightedness, they would also
have to possess information on the prices facing
individual consumers, their indifference curves for
different mixes of commodities and the relative fixity
of taste. The level of information presupposed in adjust-
ing for variations in welfare function is therefore
enormous. Hence some way has to be found out of the
impasse of basing distributive principles solely on
welfare, since the task of distributing welfare is an
impossible one for any public body or agency.

One way out of the difficulty is to extend the list
of primary goods to include special services or cash
compensation for clearly-defined cases of need, as well
as the usual benefits of income and wealth. This would
preserve the public character of primary goods comparisons, whilst meeting the objection that basing
distributive policies on a narrow list of primary goods
fails properly to take into account variations in
individual circumstances. For example, in the case of
the handicapped person, it would be possible to make a
public policy commitment to compensate for the loss of
welfare the person incurs, by providing special services
or cash compensation to a specified value to cover the
extra need for such things as transport. In general,
if people do have special needs which, it is agreed, do
lower welfare levels, then special services or resources
could be provided to meet the needs in question. These
special services may then be added to the, rather ascetic,

primary goods list of income and wealth in order to
provide a more comprehensive list of benefits to be
covered by distributive recommendations. Having
access to services designed to cope with specified
cases of need will, therefore, be a benefit to be
distributed under the principles of social justice.

If one asks for a detailed specification of those
services and benefits which ought to be included in an
extended list of primary goods, there is a strong case
for saying that many of the services and benefits
currently provided under social policy programmes should
be on the list. Extending the list in this way would
add the following benefits to the list of primary
goods: social security payments, education, health and
personal social services, and some special provision for
housing. The general reason for selecting these benefits
is that a deficiency with respect to any one of them
will probably entail a person experiencing a lower level
of welfare than someone on a similar income. Moreover,
the inclusion of these particular benefits in the list
of primary goods may be more important the less easy
it is for society to manipulate the distribution of
income. If the absence of such benefits is conventionally
accepted as giving rise to serious deficiencies in
welfare, then there will be grounds for including the
above in the list of primary goods. In other words,
end-state principles ought not only to be defined over an
appropriate distribution of income and wealth, but also
over an appropriate distribution of social services
provision. This extension in the scope of distributive
principles flows directly from the principle of
equalising welfare, which is not sufficiently implemented
simply by concentrating on income and wealth.

In order to cope with the objection that primary good
comparisons ignore special cases of need, it is therefore
necessary to extend the list of primary goods, by in-
corporating into their definition some of those
benefits currently provided by social welfare programmes.
Yet, at this point, it is reasonable to ask what sort
of claim is entailed by this conclusion. Are primary
goods comparisons to be *substituted* for welfare
comparisons or are they to be taken as *evidence* for
such comparisons because there are such severe practical
difficulties in implementing a principle of equal welfare?
The second of these interpretations seems the right one
for a number of reasons. First, even if one accepts
that social policy benefits, at least of some type, are
properly included in a list of primary goods, it does
not follow that all such benefits are properly so

listed: to discriminate among social benefits requires
a criterion more fundamental in character than that
provided within the theory of primary goods, and such
a criterion can only be based on welfare considerations.
Second, even if social benefits are properly listed as
primary goods, it does not follow that they are the
only benefits, besides income and wealth, to be so
described.   There may be a case, as I shall consider
later, for including other types of consumption within
the list of primary goods.   Finally, one wants to
avoid the suggestion, at least as much as possible,
that there is a bias towards certain patterns of life
in the theory of primary goods.   This has already
been suggested in the case of income and wealth
(Schwartz, 1973), and seems more plausible the longer
the list of primary goods becomes.   To suggest that
primary good comparisons are evidence for welfare
comparisons leaves open the possibility that a particular
set of primary good provisions is not the most efficient
way of promoting welfare because the members of a
society value more highly other types of benefit.   To
include social policy benefits within the list of
primary goods is therefore a provisional judgment which
is in principle open to revision.   In contrast, by
substituting an extended primary goods comparison for
welfare comparisons there is no logical room left for
making the appropriate revisions should they be necessary.

   Can one prescribe with any accuracy the boundary of
primary goods, and in particular are there benefits
outside the usual social service ones which ought to be
included in the list?   For instance, one possible
contender for primary goods status is the provision of
transport, particularly to those in remote or rural areas.
Raphael (1964, p. 190) suggests, for example, that
subsidised transport ought *in justice* to be provided
to those who live in such areas, to compensate them for
the disadvantages they incur, and the 1968 Transport
Act provided for transport subsidies in areas where
communities would be isolated in the event of the
current public transport being withdrawn.   There is some
intuitive support, therefore, for including transport
in the list of primary goods, and thus classifying it
as a social service.   In the present context, the question
at issue is not whether such benefits should be provided
in kind or in cash, but whether in justice they should
be provided at all, simply on the grounds that transport
is a primary good.   The organisational problem of which
is the best form to provide the benefit would follow
only if one wants to give a positive answer to the

question of whether transport should have a social service
component.

One criterion by which to distinguish primary goods
is to say that they are those benefits which are necessary
conditions for pursuing whatever ends one chooses. On
this test most social service benefits can be classified
as primary goods, whereas transport can not. On the
other hand, transport does provide the necessary
condition for carrying out a wide range of activities,
and this fact might be used as an argument in favour of
making it a primary good. The difficulty with this
argument is that people who live in rural areas have
freely chosen their place of residence, and therefore
have presumably been willing to exchange the benefits
of adequate transport in urban areas for the other
advantages which rural living brings. This in itself
seems direct evidence against including transport
among primary goods. Nor is it a good argument *for
making transport a primary good* to say that subsidies
or subsidised provision may be necessary in order to
persuade essential farm workers to remain on the land.
This may be a desirable aim in itself, but it rests on
the presumption that one particular group of people
need a special form of compensation, and as such cannot
be an argument for saying that transport ought generally
to be regarded as a primary good. A policy of subsidising transport to keep workers on the land may be justified
in terms of micro-economic considerations, but it does
not provide a reason for looking on transport either as
a social service or as a primary good.

There is, however, an important ambiguity in the
argument that transport should not be included
within the list of primary goods. In particular, it is
not clear whether it is excluded because the absence of
transport in rural areas is not counted as a net welfare
drop, on the grounds that people have freely opted for
a rural life even with its disadvantages, or whether it
is excluded on the grounds that there is a net welfare
drop in rural living, as compared with urban amenities,
but that one judges this is not a drop for which
compensation should be made. The first of these arguments
appears to be the strongest, and also one which is
applicable in the case of transport. However, the
second is also important, since any theory which restricts
the scope of public policy to redistribution over primary
goods implies that there are some variations in welfare
function for which compensation will not be paid. Not
all variations in welfare levels will give rise to
justified claims on available resources. For example,

we may take the case not of a sick or handicapped person
who experiences a lower level of welfare than the healthy
person, but of the sensitive aesthete who, pound for
pound, gains a lower level of satisfaction from his
income than his less sensitive fellow citizen. Where
other men are satisfied with fish and chips, the aesthete
may only be satisfied with caviare. The aesthete's
welfare function may give him a lower level of welfare
than other people on the same income, but is this in
itself a reason for undertaking redistributive transfers
in his favour? And, if not, how is this case to be
distinguished from the cases of medical need or
family responsibilities?

The problem has been obscured by the assertion of
some economists (e.g., Robbins, 1932, p. 132) that interpersonal comparisons of welfare were themselves value
judgments. From this assumption it is all too easy to
jump to the conclusion that if I judge A's welfare to be
lower than B's, this in itself gives an egalitarian
reason for redistribution in favour of A. But this line
of reasoning collapses together two quite separate points,
namely whether A's welfare is lower than B's, and, if so,
whether a redistribution should take place between A and
B. To believe that we can give an affirmative answer to
the first question, by basing our assessment of welfare
on, for example, psychological generalisations, is not
to imply an affirmative answer to the second question.
Thus, even if we agree with Harsanyi (1955, p. 282) that
'interpersonal comparisons of utility are not value
judgments based on some ethical or political postulates
but rather are factual propositions based on certain
principles of inductive logic', we still may want to
discriminate between some welfare variations and others,
when we come to make redistributive transfers.

Thus we can properly ask: why does sickness give
grounds for redistribution and not an aesthetic
temperament? In answer to this question, I think it is
possible to give three replies. The first is that the
degree of deprivation suffered through a deficiency in
social policy goods is likely to be that much greater
than that caused by an aesthetic sensibility. The
person who is sick or handicapped is prevented from
undertaking a greater range of activity than the
sensitive person. Second, the sort of variation in
welfare function which is covered by the concept of
'needs' is likely to be more widespread among the
population at large, and compensation for differences
in welfare function is to that extent a matter of more
urgent political priority. In addition, the government

will be in a better position to assess the degree of
welfare deficiency in some types of case, and by
concentrating on certain welfare deficiencies it cuts
its information costs. In particular, variations of
welfare function due to handicap or sickness are more
clearly associated with specific social groups than are
variations due to factors like an aesthetic temperament.
Not only is the criterion of selection more public
itself, but it can be applied in practice on a systematic
basis. Third, those variations in welfare function which
have been identified as social service needs simply
are those which are rated by the populations of
democratic welfare states as significant for public
policy. (3) None of these reasons is absolutely
knock-down, and it is in the nature of the case that they
should not be. (Think of how far cosmetic dentistry
should be allowed on the NHS for example.) However,
they are sufficient, I think, to allow us to continue
to examine the relation between equality and social
policy on the assumption that some social policy
provision is an essential element in any egalitarian
strategy.

One interesting implication of the above argument may
be worth pointing out. If we say that not all variations
in individual welfare functions are grounds for redistributive transfers, then whether a personal
characteristic is *relevant* to a person securing equality
will itself be an evaluative matter (*pace* Williams, 1962,
p. 113). It is of course true, as Williams suggests,
that to discriminate on grounds of colour between two
people is to discriminate in terms which are no more
rational than discriminating by the first letter of
somebody's name. However, the fact that some personal
characteristics are irrelevantly invoked to justify
inequality does not show that the relevance of other
personal characteristics to the justification of equality
is not in itself an evaluative matter. As between the
handicapped person and the aesthete, for example, to
say that one variation in welfare function provides
grounds for redistribution, and the other variation is
irrelevant to such transfers involves an irreducibly
evaluative judgment. I have suggested reasons as to
why certain variations in welfare function should matter
more than others; but I have no doubt that discriminating
between benefits in this way involves a set of value
judgments, albeit ones which are widely shared. (4)

2   COMPENSATION AND WELFARE

Social policy goods have been identified as the essential
components of an egalitarian approach to the distribution
of welfare. The needs which they meet are selected as
those which will license redistributive transfers, so
that special allocations of resources will be made to
compensate for specific variations in welfare function.
For expository purposes and to simplify matters, I shall
assume in this section what I later argue for, namely
that some types of redistribution are appropriately
made in kind. Using this as a basis I wish to discuss
the alleged paternalism of egalitarians. I assume that
some redistributions are made in kind for expository
purposes only: any allocation of resources tied to
specific purposes will do as well. The problems of
paternalism are, however, clearer to see in the case
where redistribution takes the form of the government
providing a specific service like the NHS, or provision
in the personal social services. I also assume that
the problems of welfare compensation occur in the context
of a just distribution of income and wealth. This enables
one to concentrate upon the problem of paternalism, since
the argument is less clouded by pragmatic considerations
concerning the decline in the quality of social services
if certain people cease to use them (cf. chapter 6.5).

One feature of utility theory is the way in which one
good can be substituted for another, and still give rise
to the same satisfaction. A person may thus enjoy equal
levels of welfare, although receiving different baskets
of goods, because he regards these different commodity
bundles as equivalent compensation for one another.
Why can the same not be true with respect to social-
policy goods? Why does the government have to compensate
people for welfare deficiencies in kind?

Successfully to question the assumption that welfare
compensation has to be made in kind, threatens to
undermine the argument so far that social-policy provision
is essential to an egalitarian strategy. It would be
possible to meet it with several practical arguments.
For example, in providing transfers in kind the link-up
is more direct with the causes of the welfare need, and
there is less chance of deception for this reason (cf.
Sen, 1973, p. 73). Moreover, there would be administrative difficulties in assessing the appropriate cash
compensation. On the other hand, a person might
complain that he was being forced, via taxation, to
spend too much of his income on the social services,
when he would prefer to spend it on other items. Is

there any reason, in principle, why his expenditure should be skewed in this way?

Before answering this question it is important to make a distinction between taxation when it is being used to redistribute benefits and taxation which gives access to state-provided goods to the same people who pay the tax. In practice these two types of taxation are mixed up (cf. Brittan, 1969, pp. 121-2), but conceptually they are quite distinct. There is a large difference between a man paying x per cent of his income in taxation as a way of providing benefits for himself, and a man paying x per cent of his income in order to finance expenditure of people who would otherwise be at a lower level of welfare. (5) Similarly, there is a great difference between a person who enjoys a public service, like the NHS, which is financed by others and the same person enjoying a public service financed by himself. The question at issue can therefore be broken down into two parts:

(a)   Should the beneficiaries of redistributive taxation be allowed to claim welfare compensation in a different form from that provided by state social policy?

(b)   Should those purchasing services out of their own pockets from the state be able to opt for lower levels of social services than would be provided by a paternalistically motivated legislator?

In question (a) the assumption is that a person might be able to claim compensation for a variation in individual welfare function not because he was being compensated for a publicly-recognised welfare deficiency, but because he was prepared to forego the compensation of publicly-recognised deficiencies in exchange for compensation of other welfare deficiencies which were not publicly-recognised. The sensitive aesthete, for example, might prefer a subsidised opera-seat in exchange for the benefits of health insurance.

In answer to (a) it is superficially appealing to answer that people should be able to make the choice. For example, if a person with poor health risks says that he is prepared to forego the redistributed benefits he enjoys under the NHS by way of available health care, then why should he not be allowed to take equivalent cash or other compensation instead? After all, if *he* regards it as compensation for the health care he risks losing, then it seems as though his welfare level will not drop.

I do not want to rely on the argument here that, from

the point of view of his own interests, he may be making
the wrong choice. This again would be a straight
paternalist argument, and on the whole I want to reject
the paternalist impulse in social policy on the grounds
that it is incompatible with the equal respect owed to
men as rational, deliberating agents. However, there
is an argument for insisting that the person should
take the service in kind, or not at all. This is
simply that the reason for making the transfer in the
first place is that the person is judged deficient in
welfare because he does not have access to certain social
policy goods. The reason for making the redistribution
is to improve his level of welfare, where this welfare
level is judged lower than other people's on the grounds
that he lacks a certain commodity. If the person then
judges that his welfare is not lower than other
people's despite his lacking that commodity, the whole
rationale of the redistribution disappears, and there
is no reason for making a transfer of any kind. To
have a public rule for the redistribution of benefits
means that a person will be only entitled to the
benefits if he satisfies the conditions of the rule.
Hence to have a rule, which bases itself on the fact that
people have lower welfare for specific reasons, means
that in order to qualify for the benefit people ought
to satisfy the conditions of eligibility entailed by
those reasons.

This point touches on a more general argument about
the redistributive impact of the welfare state. It is
sometimes argued that the welfare state, and social
policy measures in particular, are not redistributive
because too much money goes to people who *do* the welfare,
and not enough to those who *receive* it. Where this
is not just a slightly more sophisticated version of the
claim that bureaucrats waste money, it must rest on a
claim about compensation. In particular, it must presuppose that the people receiving the benefits of goods
in kind would enjoy the same level of welfare if they
were given the monetary equivalent of the costs of the
service to them. But the whole point of providing a
service like the NHS is to provide people with a benefit
which matches variations in individual welfare functions,
even when there is an equal distribution of income. The
service, including personnel is what is being provided,
and if there were not the need for the service, there
would be no reason to make any transfers.

There is a particular case where this reply may not
hold, and where there may be some substance in the
claim that too much money goes on providing the service

to the detriment of the client. This is in certain
instances in the personal social services where social
workers are assigned to a family in order to help them
overcome the problems of 'secondary' poverty, when in
fact the family's problems spring from 'primary'
poverty. (6) There may well be cases in which this
happens, and where the family concerned would not
only enjoy the benefits of a higher income, but would
also avoid the indignity of having someone else manage
their affairs if the problem of primary poverty were
met. However, unless it is simply assumed, as a matter
of fact, that there are no cases of secondary poverty,
then the general argument collapses. For, again, the
point of providing professional social work is to
provide a specific service. If the appropriate variation
in welfare function is accepted as being a legitimate
ground for providing trained support, then it should
provide the only basis on which equivalent redistribution should take place.

This still leaves the second part of the original
question: should those purchasing state services out of
their own pockets be allowed to choose a lower level of
service than would be provided by a paternalistically
motivated legislator? Within our present tax and welfare
system, it is extremely difficult to isolate such a
person, simply because the provision of public services
and the redistributive impact of taxation are so inter-
related. However, the example I have in mind is a person
who is paying, via taxation, his contribution towards
redistribution and is also paying to cover the welfare
services he uses. He is prepared to accept a lower
standard of welfare service for himself in exchange for
a lower tax bill, and at the same time is quite prepared
to continue to make his contribution towards redistribution.

The legislator may well believe that the person's
welfare level will be lower if he accepts poorer welfare
services. Does the person not have the right, however,
voluntarily to reduce his own welfare below a specified
equal standard? Or does the legislator, under the
principle of equality, have the right to force the
person to consume a higher level of welfare services?
My own answer to these questions is that the paternalistic
impulse should be rejected, and that anybody has the right
to reduce their own level of welfare below the average
of the community at large, if this is the result of their
own choice. To override somebody's wishes in this
respect is to fail to recognise the equal right to
freedom, which is secured by the first principle of

Rawlsian social justice. (7)   And this is to fail in
recognising him as an equal, in the sense of his being
an agent with his own purposes and interests, and his
own conception of what those purposes and interests are.

The practical argument is sometimes used here that
society will not subsequently allow a person to suffer
or to be harmed, if it becomes clear that he has made
the wrong choice in withdrawing from the state-provided
service. It will provide the service in any case,
whether or not the person has an historic entitlement.
In such an example, the person will derive the value of
the benefit, as well as the increased income he enjoyed
previously. However, even this practical argument is
not decisive in all cases, or circumstances. It may be
possible to charge the person for service, or for the
actuarial equivalent of the service. Moreover, the fact
that a service may be socially provided on grounds of
humanity or benevolence is no reason for saying that a
person has, in justice, an entitlement to the service.

The other practical argument against individual with-
drawal from welfare services is that there are often
taxpayers who are meeting part of the costs of the
services who are not themselves able to forego the
benefits. The clearest example here is corporate bodies
paying sales' or profits' taxes, where part of the
revenue is used to finance the social services. However,
this is not a strong argument against individual with-
drawal. All we need to assume is that the person who
withdraws from the service only takes in compensation
the value of his own contribution to his own needs, net
of any redistributive payments he makes and net of any
general supplementation the welfare service derives
from taxation on those other than individual taxpayers.

The general conclusion of this section, therefore, is
to say that it is not permissible for beneficiaries of
certain redistributive transfers to substitute a
particular benefit they are receiving for something else,
but that it is permissible for people to withdraw from
certain social-service schemes taking in compensation
their contribution to their own use of the scheme. The
latter conclusion should hold, even when it may mean
the person concerned experiences a consequently lower
level of welfare.

3 EQUALITY AND TRANSFERS IN KIND

In the previous section I argued for the legitimacy of
tying certain types of transfers to particular uses.

In this section I shall continue to assume that some of
these transfers should be provided in kind, and I shall
discuss some problems of political choice which arise
when equality of provision is made an aim of such
transfers.

If transfers in kind are primary goods, then the
egalitarian holds that their provision should be equalised
in order to produce an equal distribution of welfare.
In practice this requirement comes to mean that people
should be secured equal access to the health, education
and personal social services. In fact, with respect to
regional inequalities in the provision of these services
there has been a wide degree of political consensus on
the desirability of reducing disparities in their
distribution. (8) For example, equality has been
explicitly adopted in the formula for working out the
RSG to local authorities and in the RHA formula for
resource allocation to different regions in the NHS.

The usual method for measuring equality of access has
been in terms of indicators related to the input of
resources. In the NHS for example Cooper and Culyer
(1972, pp. 55-7) have suggested such variables as the
following as appropriate indicators: the population of
an area per GP; staffed hospital beds per 1000 of the
population; expenditure per in-patient week on staff as
a percentage of the national mean; and the percentage
of consultants by their speciality per million of the
population.

The use of such indicators has been criticised because
they are only measures of input and not of output.
Ideally the aim should be to distribute health services
in such a way that morbidity and mortality rates were
equalised throughout the population. In practice it is
impossible to show a link between health services and the
appropriate output indicators, since so many other factors
intervene. (9) In the absence of any coherent model, by
which health services could be related to sickness rates,
etc., one will just have to be content with the aim of
equality of access as measured by the appropriate
indicators. At least within a service pursuing this aim
one avoids the problems of ignominy and social inequality
which were associated with the old division between
private and 'panel' patients.

However, even when one accepts this limited aim
problems arise. A particular difficulty is that the
pursuit of equality may well involve the cushioning of
administrative inefficiency, with consequently lower
minimum standards of service than would otherwise obtain.
For example, within the RHA allocation formula case-flow

is used as an indicator for determining the allocation of
resources. Yet the rate of case-flow may depend as much
on the way that resources are utilised as on the level
of resources which are available. It is known for
example that there are inexplicable variations in
practice between hospital regions in the number of
post-operative convalescent days allowed in the hernia
patients (Cooper, 1975, p. 56). Since effective treatment
does not appear to depend on a long post-operative period
in hospital, this suggests that regions with a faster
case-flow are using their available resources more
efficiently, with a consequent improvement in standards.

Paradoxically, the actual formula which is used in
the NHS to allocate regional funds may reward efficiency,
even though it has the aim of promoting equality. To
see how this result arises, we may consider the following
hypothetical example. In two regions A and B, we can
suppose equal populations, equal morbidity and mortality
ratios, and an equal stock of equipment and labour, as
well as equal levels in the quality of care. However,
if region A is more efficient than B, then its case-flow
will be greater than B's (cf. West, 1973, pp. 163-4).
The RHA formula will provide A with more resources than
B, because of the case-flow element in the calculation
of entitlement. From the viewpoint of efficiency this
may well be justified, but it has the result of *increasing*
rather than *decreasing* regional inequalities. From the
viewpoint of equality, given an administrative unit which
produces a slower case-flow for the same inputs, the
correct solution would be to increase the financial
inputs to the less efficient regions in order to produce
similar levels of case output. Yet a desire to raise
minimum standards in the long run may well dictate a
policy of rewarding efficiency and penalising inefficiency
i.e., of providing more financial inputs to those regions
with greater productivity. (10)

This is a more specific example of the familiar
conflict which may arise between equality and efficiency,
and which I have already discussed in general terms
(chapter 3.3). Theoretically the optimum solution is
for the policy-maker to determine his relative preference
for equality as against the raising of minimum standards
and to choose that 'mix' of policy options which
maximises the combined benefits. The procedure is for
the policy maker to determine his own schedule of
preferences, which can be represented by an indifference
curve, and for him also to determine the feasible
combinations of equality and efficiency. The optimum
mix of policies occurs at the point where the tangent

of the indifference curve and feasibility curve defines
the appropriate levels of each policy. However, this
optimum solution may be unattainable for a number of
reasons. Even if the policy-maker can define a suitable
preference schedule, a task which is difficult enough
in itself, it needs to be shown that the policy-maker's
indifference curve over equality and efficiency satisfies
the requirements for a point of tangency to emerge in
relation to the technically possible combinations of
policies following on the two goals. There is, however,
no reason to think that this condition will always be
satisfied. The technically possible mix of policies
in particular may not satisfy the appropriate requirements:
for instance, there may be no perfect divisibility
between efficiency and equality. Efficiency gains may
come in 'lumps' with wide ranges of efficiency compatible
with the same degree of equality in allocation. In such
a situation the policy-maker clearly needs a 'second
best' solution, without having any clear guidance as to
how he might achieve one.

From this discussion two major problems, associated
with the pursuit of equality concerning transfers in
kind, emerge. There is first the difficulty of defining
an appropriate basis on which to judge whether the aim
of promoting equal welfare is being satisfied; and there
is second the problem of the political trade-offs which
have to be made with other values. The first of these
problems could arise with any end-state principle whose
scope was determined over the specific primary goods I
have listed. The second problem is more directly
connected with equality, and underlines the point that
policy conflicts based on competing values may arise not
only at the macro level, where it may be a matter of
trading-off the benefits of economic growth against
equality, but also at the micro level, where within
organisations, analogous problems may arise.

4   PENSIONS AND REDISTRIBUTION

In the previous section I looked at primary goods
transferred in kind, and interpreted the application of
the principle of equal welfare in terms of equal access
to a set of services. However, also included within
the extended list of primary goods were social security
payments. In this section I shall examine in more
detail the rationale for including such payments as
primary goods to be provided by public policy, and I
shall discuss one of the policy problems which arises

in consequence. To simplify the discussion I shall
concentrate upon one particular type of payment, namely
retirement pensions, but much of the argument has a
natural extension to cases like sickness and invalidity
benefits.

I have chosen the example of pensions for four
specific reasons.

1 With pensions the problem of distribution does
not concern a clean-sheet situation, but a case where
individuals and households have acquired expectations
of unequal welfare.

2 There is a special problem for the egalitarian in
defining the appropriate reference group within which
to apply his distributive principles.

3 The problem of savings and their treatment is
extremely pressing in the case of pensions.

4 In the last few years a number of white papers
(e.g. DHSS, 1969; 1971) have been published on pensions'
policy, and they provide a convenient focal point for
discussing the problems of political choice which occur
in this area of public policy.

The first three of these considerations are important
in bringing out the complications that can arise when
the principle of equality is applied to a specific
policy area, and the government white papers provide
an illustration of how the egalitarian theory of justice
may be used to evaluate public policy proposals.

There is, however, a problem as to whether the
provision of retirement income should be considered a
primary good in any case. The general reason advanced
above for augmenting the primary goods of income and
wealth is that welfare variations may arise for people
on the same income, and that a number of the sources of
these variations are of such character as to give rise
to justified claims for compensation. However, it
might be argued in the present case that, in as much as
people faced different and worse prospects of retirement
income, this should not create an entitlement to income
supplementation. Retirement income, on this argument,
should be a matter of personal savings, and should
not be a primary good which society has an interest in
distributing in a certain way. To raise questions
about the distribution of retirement income as a primary
good might seem, therefore, to pre-judge the issue of
whether it should be so treated. If people choose to
save different amounts for their retirement, then the
deferment of present consumption by some people would
seem to justify their prospects of better retirement
income in the future.

A further advantage of basing retirement income on savings is that it underlines the place of individual self reliance and forethought in the provisions people make for the contingencies of their lives. The development of these personal qualities is often thought to be essential to the satisfactory working of a free market economy. (11) On the other hand, it is possible to argue that these factors ought not to be important until one has secured an adequate initial distribution of resources, and this is extremely difficult to do if one ties potential retirement income to people's income during their working lives. If this latter income is unfairly distributed, according to any particular criterion, then retirement income, under the savings model, will be unfairly distributed, since it will be a function of earned income.

A further disadvantage with the savings principle is that it is actuarially based, and is unresponsive therefore to welfare considerations. An example of what this means is provided by the treatment of female pension rights in the 1971 white paper. In the proposed guidelines for private occupational pension schemes laid down in 'Strategy for Pensions' (DHSS, 1971) the minimum acceptable level of pension is allowed to be lower for a woman than for a man. The justification offered for this provision is, 'to take account of the fact that pension [sic] must be available to them from the age of 60 (compared with 65 for men) and their greater longevity, with an offset to allow for the absence of mandatory dependency provision.' (DHSS, 1971, p. 17). Allowing the standards to drop in this way is clearly the result of adopting actuarial principles. Yet it is perfectly intelligible to hold that women should enjoy the same income as men without suffering a drop in their pension entitlement, as is the case if their pension assessment is made on actuarial grounds. Indeed given life-expectancy is longer for a woman, it may be argued that with a longer period of retirement women have greater needs than men, because they experience a longer period of dependency. One major objection to the proposals outlined in 'Strategy' is that they build into pension arrangements certain principles of distribution without allowing for an institutional mechanism which would leave the possibility of other principles being used to revise the distribution of pensioner income. To adopt actuarial principles in calculating pensions must entail, given present life-expectancy rates for men and women, inequality in pension entitlement. Hence the real question is whether it is desirable, on grounds of both equity and equality, to adopt such actuarialy-based pension financing. The answer to that question is assumed rather than argued for in 'Strategy for Pensions', and in the savings model generally.

If retirement incomes are treated as a primary good, then they will be based on the pay-as-you-go principle which has a different rationale from that of the savings model. By this principle, the social security system becomes the mechanism by which society settles the issue of intergenerational (worker - non-worker) income distribution through the political process rather than leaving its resolution to the market and private decisions. Samuelson (1958) has shown that once we exclude the savings process we can no longer understand the intergenerational distribution of consumption on a market model. If we suppose that retirement consumption is financed by an agreement between one generation and younger generations, under which the middle aged transfer some of their consumption to the young in exchange for support in old age, the free market will not tend to an optimum - indeed such an exchange process would not be viable at all. In order that generations may enjoy positive consumption in old age, they will have to come to an intergenerational contract, under which the currently productive members of the population support the retired on the understanding that yet unborn generations will support them on retirement. A contract of this sort will allow the optimum rate of inter-generational transfers to arise. (12)

If both the savings principle and the market method are rejected as unsuitable methods for the financing of retirement income, then the only appropriate institutional framework will be based on the pay-as-you-go principle backed by the political process. Indeed such an institutional framework can be regarded as reflecting an implicit social contract under which present working generations agree to finance the consumption of the elderly in exchange for an agreement by the next genera-tion to finance their consumption. Moreover, if the social security system is not actuarially based, it will reflect the sort of contractual agreement outlined in the previous chapter, under which the contracting parties agree to compensate the less fortunate or talented by providing them with resources they could not otherwise obtain.

However, if responsibility for retirement income is to be devolved upon the political process, then this raises the important issue of the appropriate principles

upon which retirement income should be distributed.
There is a strong case for saying that equality is the
appropriate principle, since justifications for
alternative distributions are less relevant in this
particular case than they are to situations when
income inequality might be justified. Since pensioners
are no longer working, they no longer make differential
contributions to the social product, so that there is
no case for making incomes proportional to marginal
contribution. An appropriate principle, for example,
might be to pay flat-rate pensions at some specified
fraction of average disposable incomes, the argument for
not equating the two being that some off-set should be
made to compensate for travelling costs and other
expenses connected with work. Against the equality
principle, however, there is a case for saying that
pensions should be graduated according to previous
income. The main argument here is that in a situation
of unequal income distribution, people acquire conventional expectations of a certain level of welfare. To
opt for equality may involve running against these
conventional expectations. Sidgwick pointed out that
considerations based on maintaining conventional
expectations were likely to provide intuitive reasons
against 'an ideal system of rules of distribution'. (13)
Any social security system which is based on the pay-
as-you-go principle is liable therefore to represent a
compromise between these two sets of considerations,
and the usual form the reconciliation takes is to modify
the payment of graduated benefits by some redistribution
in favour of the worst-off group.

It may also be worth mentioning one practical
advantage of the pay-as-you-go principle, namely its
flexibility in dealing with the conflicting considerations
of equality and conventional expectations. Basing
pensions' policy on a pay-as-you-go basis means that the
benefit formulas may be changed in accordance with
competing views on a fair distribution. In the nature
of the case this is impossible to do in the savings
model.

Under a pay-as-you-go system there is no reason why
the basic pension provision should not be supplemented
by private savings. I have defined the principle of
equal welfare so that it requires equal mean levels of
welfare averaged over a person's life-time, rather than
an equal distribution of welfare at all times. Accumulated wealth from savings would therefore be permissible
under the principle of equality provided that it was
financed from a distribution of resources which was

itself just.   Consequently, if a person is prepared to
incur a lower level of welfare during his working life
in order to enjoy a correspondingly higher level of
welfare on retirement, there is no reason under the
principle of equality why he should be prevented from
doing so.

On general points connected with the level of pensions
it is probably worth noting that the egalitarian should
logically favour the taxation of retirement income from
all sources, including state pensions. The rationale
for this is that benefits are income just like any
other, and there is no special reason for exempting
these particular forms of income from tax. In general
the available data (drawn from the USA) shows that the
budget needs of the aged are no greater than those of
younger tax-payers (Pechman et al., 1968, pp. 83 and
202). This is particularly so in a social service
system which covers health costs, which are often a
potentially large item in retired peoples' budgets.
Indeed because the old often hold forms of accumulated
wealth, owner-occupied houses being the most conspicuous
example, their budget needs may be smaller in some
respects than the young. There are no special reasons
on welfare grounds, therefore, for exempting the old
from taxation. Non-exemption would also prove advantageous from the point of view of raising minimum
pension levels, and thereby improving the distribution
of benefits. A major difficulty with raising minimum
benefits under the present NI scheme is that improved
benefit rates also go in full to retired people with
high incomes. To spread benefits in this way means
there is less available for pensioners with low incomes.
By taxing retirement incomes from all sources, this
would not only cope with the anomaly of having some
relatively high incomes free of tax, but would also
provide greater funds for raising minimum levels of
benefit.

The chief argument against this proposal is that it
would involve very large administrative costs, particularly to process the income tax receipts of those
retired people who pay little tax. At least one
government, however, has contemplated with equanimity
the prospect of making such benefits taxable. (14)
Meanwhile, until this objective is achieved, there is
a strong argument for resisting those many calls for
exempting ever larger slices of pensioners' *earned*
income from taxation.

5   Need and equality

1 THE CONCEPT OF NEED

Distribution according to need is often associated with
the principle of equality. Commenting on the opinion
that the welfare state had not succeeded in reducing
inequalities, Thompson (1958) argued that the post war
growth of the social services had made a significant
impact upon the reduction of inequalities because there
were now a number of goods which were distributed 'on
need, and not on ability to pay'. At a rather higher
level of abstraction Marx (1875, p. 23) argued that
distribution on the basis of need would be characteristic
of a fully developed communist society, in which there
was full economic and social equality. At least in some
political arguments, therefore, the assumption is made
that to distribute according to need is to satisfy the
claims of equality. In this chapter I consider the
argument that the needs principle is equivalent to the
equality principle, and offer a formulation of the
former which can be used in social policy contexts.
However, before discussing the relationship between
distribution according to need and the principle of
equality, it is important to be clear on the concept of
need itself.
    The primitive and common notion underlying all uses
of the term 'need' is that of a necessary condition
for the attainment of a specified end-state. Thus, if
a car needs petrol in order to run, then this simply
means that petrol is a necessary condition for the car's
effective performance. It is for this reason that it
is always sensible, whenever someone says 'x is needed',
to ask: for what purposes? (Barry, 1965, p. 48;
Minogue, 1963, p. 104). The simple specification of a
need, then, is always the stipulation of a necessary

condition for some end-state, which may or may not be
regarded as desirable by the speaker. For example, if
I say of my opponent in tennis that he needs to win the
next three games in order to win the set, I am stating
the condition he must fulfil if he is going to be
successful in this respect, but there may be no implication that I want him to win the games - quite the
contrary. From the most general meaning of need
therefore, it seems that it is important to decide on
the merits of the end-state implied by any stipulation
of need.

However, in political arguments people sometimes
use the concept of need without specifying the end-state
to which it is conducive, and therefore without justifying that end-state in terms of some distinct distributive
value. This may be just linguistic slackness, of course.
On the other hand, I am inclined to think that it is a
particular usage of the term 'need' in its own right,
and that in this usage the concept can be given
determinate sense. When people speak about needs in
the abstract, they may be interpreted as referring to
those goods and services which it is rational to want
as the necessary conditions for any given level of
welfare. In this sense needs can be identified with the
notion of primary goods, which are the means to welfare.
I have already given reasons in the last chapter for
extending the list of Rawlsian primary goods to include
social service benefits, and this seems to tie in with
the concept of needs, since social policy goods are
sometimes regarded as needs in this general sense. On
this definition, therefore, if we say that A has greater
needs than B, we simply mean that A needs a larger set
of primary goods than does B in order to achieve the
same level of welfare. The concept of need is still
identified with the concept of a necessary condition,
but in this case it is equated with a necessary
condition of a specified level of welfare.

To say that distribution should be according to need
involves therefore two distinct claims:
(a)   there are some benefits which can be regarded as
      primary goods;
(b)   the distribution of resources ought to be such as
      to rectify any deficiencies with respect to these
      primary goods.
With regard to the first part of this claim it seems
unexceptionable to identify primary goods as needs,
since this is entailed by the definition of primary
goods as the necessary conditions of welfare. The
problem lies in the second part of the claim. How

satisfactory a distributive principle is it to say
that a simple deficiency of primary goods should form
the basis of allocation? What is the relationship,
moreover, between this principle and the principle of
equality?

2   NEED AND EQUALITY

Vlastos has argued (1962, p. 40) that distribution by
need 'is in fact the most perfect form of equality'.
I shall express this claim as the thesis that the needs
principle is extensionally equivalent to the equality
principle. In suggesting the principles are extensionally
equivalent the claim is that, although their meaning
is distinct, their application to distributive questions
would in fact result in an identical distribution. (1)
Any distribution obtained by applying the one principle
would be obtained by applying the other. The reason
for requiring them to be *extensionally* equivalent is
that, if they are only equivalent intensionally, the
claim to equivalence becomes trivial. Distribution by
need may be defined in terms of equality, but then it
would be of no interest that the two principles yielded
identical distributions.
    Vlastos supports the case for extensional equivalence
by appeal to the following example. Suppose someone's
life has been threatened, and as a result he asks for
extra police protection. We may assume that everyone
else in the community is receiving an equal level of
protection from the police force. In asking for extra
protection, the threatened individual may be making a
claim on resources which is greater than that of other
people. However, the extra resources used in protecting
him bring up his security level only to a standard equal
to that of everybody else. If we say that the threatened
person needed extra police protection, it would seem that
the satisfaction of that need results in an equality,
namely maintaining a person's equal right to life.
What the egalitarian wants is equal levels of benefit,
rather than an equal distribution of resources, and in
this case such a distribution of benefits seems to
result from a distributing certain goods or resources
according to need. Hence need and equality yield the
same distribution: therefore they are extensionally
equivalent principles.
    The example is intended to clinch the argument for
the extensional equivalence. However, it seems to
work to the opposite effect, and it is worth examining

to see why. It is of course true that the threatened
person who gains extra police protection has had his
need satisfied to *extra protection up to the level of
everybody else*. However, this does not imply that his
need for police protection has been satisfied *per se*.
All members of the community might need extra police
protection in the sense that they would benefit from the
lower level of risk that this would bring. The same
will be true of each individual in the community: he
would benefit from more police protection in the sense
that his right to life would be more secure. All that
has been satisfied in the example are needs up to an
equal level of benefit, not needs as such. Presumably
needs as such would only be completely satisfied when
personal security was certain for every member of the
community.

To illustrate the point consider a further development
of the same example. Let us suppose that police resources
are distributed so as to secure an equal level of
protection for each individual in the community. However,
the protection is not fool-proof: some people will be
mugged or shot despite policy activity. General standards
of security in the community could be increased but only
at a very large extra cost. However, there are some
resources available which would improve protection for
some people but not for all. If these resources were
spent to the benefit of a minority of the population, we
should surely say that their need for improved security
had been met without implying that everyone else
benefited to the same degree. In other words, we can
satisfy some people's need for personal security by
reducing the risks they run, but this does not imply
that all people in their community will derive a similar
benefit. The point here is that the satisfaction of
needs is itself a benefit to be distributed in accordance
with some principle, and this means that the principle
of satisfying needs is on a distinct logical level from
the principle of equality. They are extensionally
*in*equivalent principles because they refer to different
stages of policy judgment: the needs principle picks
out which benefits are to be distributed and the equality
principle determines the correct allocation of these
benefits. (2)

The plausibility of the extensional equivalence view
seems to derive from an implicit assumption that the
appropriate end-state from which to view the claims of
need is equality. But this is to build an intensional
equivalence with equality from the beginning. Once
we allow that there are needs whose satisfaction would

results in inequality, because other people have similar
but unsatisfied needs, then the distinct scope of the
principles can be clearly seen.

3   THE BOUNDARIES OF NEED CLAIMS

One difficulty with using the concept of need in
distributive contexts is that the amount of unsatisfied
need appears to be virtually infinite. In particular
this is a problem for social policy. There are a number
of reasons for this. Rising expectations of health and
educational standards have lead to a greater demand for
better schools and health care. The success of schools
and hospitals in satisfying needs itself creates problems,
with expensive higher education and intensive care
facilities increasingly required by the young and the old.
Moreover, there seems to be a great deal of room for
quality improvements in both these areas, with each
successive level of investment producing a lower rate
of return. There is a political problem, therefore, in
trying to draw boundaries around need claims, in order
not to pre-empt all a society's resources for a narrow
set of purposes.
     I shall discuss this problem particularly as it
affects health services, though what I have to say
applies, I think, equally to the personal social services.
I choose this particular field for two reasons. First,
the concept of need seems more at home in health services
than in an area like education, where, although the
concept of need is sometimes used, the allocation of
resources is not so obviously based on an identification
of needs. Second, it is widely recognised that the
problems of allocating health care raises acute problems
of political and ethical principle and it is therefore
important to examine the implications of a principle
like that of equality, in the present context.
     In hospital management and health programmes the
apparent infinity of needs has led to dramatic calls to
'ration' health care. Once the fallacy became apparent
of assuming that free health care would make the
problems of illness and disease disappear, it was
inevitable that some mechanism would have to be found
for limiting the claims of unmet need. (3) In practice
queuing for health treatment became the most obvious·
form of rationing, but it was not the only one: lack
of capital investment and regional shortages were
others. Such rationing can be regarded as an illustration
of the fact that need is not itself a basis on which

distributive judgments can be made, but that the
satisfaction of needs is itself a benefit to be distributed in accordance with some principle. To distribute
according to need has come to mean, in some social policy
contexts at least, distribute goods in order to make
people better off. But this is not a distributive
principle; just a general assertion that society has
an obligation to improve welfare.

How should needs be satisfied in terms of the
egalitarian theory which we have been developing? I
have already argued that distribution by need is not
equivalent to the principle of equality, and generally
it seems better to look at the problem of need satisfaction in the context of seeking to promote an equal
distribution of welfare, rather than in the abstract.
The fact that medical needs are infinite means that not
all deficiencies in primary goods can be rectified.
Some people therefore will have unsatisfied needs. Now
we can define a situation of equal welfare as one in
which everyone either has an equal risk of having
unsatisfied needs, or is compensated for having a higher
level of risk. In other words the problem for the
egalitarian is not simply to satisfy needs, but also to
distribute equally the risks of unsatisfied needs (which,
in the medical case, are morbidity and mortality risks),
at a level which is socially acceptable. A situation of
equal welfare is then defined in terms of such a
distribution of risks.

The ethical appeal of this equal risks principle is
analogous to the ethical appeal of an equal welfare
principle taken to be constitutive of social justice.
The natural distribution of health risks is as arbitrary
from the moral point of view as the natural distribution
of abilities and talents. The provision of preventative
and curative facilities to counter-act the effects of
this natural lottery is justified in terms of a general
ethical predisposition in favour of the sharing of
resources. There is, moreover, a practical advantage
in focusing on health risks rather than the unsatisfied
needs which arise through a lack of adequate medical
facilities. By concentrating on existing needs large
amounts of resources may be used up by expensive medical
technology in coping with illness, when the same money
could be used for preventative purposes with better
results.

The principle of a medical risk-pool (cf. Fried,
1970) assumes that an increase in mortality or morbidity
risks is an individual cost which ought, if possible, to
be compensated. However, although in general true, the

assumption is not always valid. People may undertake
activities which increase their mortality risks above the
average, for example by climbing mountains, swimming in
rough seas or driving fast. As the principle stands,
at present, it would involve compensating people for
those extra risks, possibly at considerable social cost.
This raises the question of whether such compensation
should, in justice, be paid. Why, for example, should
the community's risk-pool bear the health costs of those
who engage in dangerous sports? In this type of case
there are no grounds for arguing that the distribution
of health risks is arbitrary from the moral point of
view, since the people who are incurring the risks
undertake the relevant activities voluntarily.

There are, of course, problems in distinguishing
what are voluntary and what are involuntary additions to
health risks. Some strictly voluntary risks may be such
a matter of established social habit that people are
hardly aware of choosing the more risky of two alternative
courses of action. Thus people may drive private cars
when it would be safer for them to use public transport,
or they may take aeroplanes rather than travel by ship.
In both these cases there is a voluntary addition to
health risks, and the relevant social practices may give
rise to a greater social cost in providing health
services, but habit and social pressures may both be
important in obscuring from people the voluntary nature
of the choices involved. Moreover, there may be uncertainty about the degree of risk which is involved in
undertaking the activity. There is enough scientific
dispute about the relationship between smoking and lung
cancer for it to be at least open to question whether
the former increases the risk of the latter, even if it
is quite clearly correlated with such risks.

If people voluntarily increase their risks of
unsatisfied health needs, there seems to be no reason
for pooling these increased risks in with those of the
general community. The practical difficulties do not
affect the question of principle. It may be difficult
in particular cases to decide whether an activity has
been voluntarily undertaken, but the resolution of this
problem has to be made by reference to the principle
of pure procedural justice. Procedural justice obtains
whenever the outcome of a procedure cannot be assessed
independently of the means by which it is arrived at.
If society uses fair procedures to decide that some
activities count as voluntary additions to health risks,
then it is fair to limit the pooling of health risks to
those activities which do not fall into the appropriate

category. That some other activities might have been
included in the same list does not make it unjust for
society to limit its subsidised medical provision only
to those cases which are judged involuntary risks. If
this argument is accepted, it will not be unjust for
society to accept an unequal distribution of unsatisfied
medical needs, provided the inequality is due to the
results of activities voluntarily undertaken.

A just distribution of health resources therefore
need not compensate for the increased health risks which
people voluntarily incur. Note, however, that there is
no reason in principle why society should paternalistically outlaw risky activities, on the grounds that their
practice increases the social cost of medicine. It could
either refuse publicly-funded medical facilities to those
who were injured as a result of their freely-chosen
activities, or it could charge the full cost-price of the
medical care which it did provide. (4) Those people who
liked mountain climbing or swimming in rough seas could
always insure themselves privately against the chance of
medical costs. A more paternalistic solution would be
to *compel* people to take out insurance whenever they
engaged in risky sports or other dangerous activities.
The disadvantage with this solution, however, is that
with many activities it would be extremely difficult to
enforce such compulsory insurance, and inequities could
soon arise between those activities which were easily
policed and those which were not.

To distribute risks equally is not to determine the
level of health risk that should be maintained. Nor
can this level be determined in the abstract original
position, since although health care is a primary good,
it is not the only good which people want. That is,
people may prefer higher mortality and morbidity risks
if this enables them to purchase other benefits. In
the original position the contracting parties are
ignorant not simply of their own tastes and preferences,
but also of the preferences of the members of the
particular society into which they will enter. They
cannot tell in advance, therefore, how much they will
value health care as against other demands on resources.
Indeed we cannot even assume that the parties in the
original position would count health services as a primary
good. All I have argued so far is that if the list of
primary goods is extended to cover health care, then the
principle of equality agreed in the original position
should apply to that particular case. However this
implies nothing about the level of health services, and
hence the level of unsatisfied need, which is acceptable.

The question of the appropriate level cannot therefore be settled from the perspective of the original position, but has to be decided by members of an existing society having known tastes and preferences. Since the risk-pool depends upon a social sharing of resources, it seems appropriate that the level of health risks should be determined by the social decision-making process, and in practice this turns out to be the political process. It is worth stressing that the social decision-making process is political, since some writers (e.g., Rothenberg, 1961, pp. 316-23) have suggested that such decision processes are based on a *consensus* of values. (5) However, in suggesting that the level of health risks be settled through the political process, there is no implication that there would be a consensus on what, for example, ought to be the level of public expenditure on health. Even if, as Rothenberg suggests, there is a consensus about the social welfare function - that is, consensus about the form the social decision process should take - this does not imply agreement on the policies that the social welfare function should select. Indeed the democratic political process is one way of arriving at a social choice in the face of individual disagreement (cf. Nath, 1968, p. 128). Policy-makers' decisions on the appropriate level of public expenditure on health services are unlikely therefore to be based on consensus concerning the policies in question; rather they will be based on the results of the political decision-making machinery.

The democratic political process, however, has a number of weaknesses, which are relevant to the question of how well it is likely to perform the task of determining satisfactorily the appropriate level of health risk in the light of community preferences. Most obviously there is the difficulty that a majority can coerce a minority into accepting a level of risk which members of the minority would not themselves choose. However, this may not be a serious problem, depending on how rational it is for each individual to exchange the benefits of freedom of choice in these matters for the benefits of belonging to a system of risk-pooling. More importantly, in the present context, the striking defect of the political process is that political parties in a competitive democratic system exercise 'full-line supply' (Breton, 1974, p. 50) over their policies, and this weakens the extent to which society, through the ballot-box, determines its own policy in these matters.

Full-line supply exists when the provider of one

good will only supply that good when other goods which
he supplies are also bought. Some computer manufacturers,
for example, will only supply computer hardware if the
buyer agrees to purchase their software as well.
Similarly, political parties in a competitive situation
do not supply discrete, single policies to the voters,
but policy bundles. The elector then has to choose which
policy bundle he prefers from those which are presented
to him, without being able to discriminate within the
bundles. It might well happen, therefore, that a
majority party has very little popular support for some
items of its policy package. Indeed its policy on
health might be that least liked by electors from those
which are presented to them, but, because this unpopular
policy has been yoked with popular policies on other
issues, the winning party is in a position to implement
its proposals. In this way the link can be cut between
democratic social choice and standard setting in
social policy.

How seriously does the fact of full-line supply
undermine the claim that the level of health risks
should be decided democratically? Potentially I believe
that it could be damagingly serious in its implications.
How serious it is practically is difficult to say for a
number of reasons. Expenditure on many items of social
policy is extremely popular in a democratic country like
Britain, and competitive political parties are therefore
more likely to use their health policy as the popular
issue with which to yoke unpopular measures than *vice
versa*. (6) Moreover it is often difficult in the social
policy field to make fast changes of policy since
expenditure commitments have to be decided in advance,
and so much of what is spent is locked-in in the short-
term on such items as staff salaries and capital
servicing. The scope for party competition is correspondingly lessened, and this may have an important
impact in diminishing the strategic usefulness of health
policies in party competition. However, one has to
admit that the social determination of the level of
health risk remains a hit-and-miss affair in many respects,
and this is part of the cost of having a system which
pools risks in order to achieve a fair balance of
unsatisfied need within the community.

In speaking about the distribution of risks so far
I have been primarily concerned with the provision of
health services to the non-permanently disabled or
handicapped. However, I assume that the principle of
equal welfare would license compensation to the handicapped in a number of forms. There would be appropriate

medical treatment, help with special transport and housing
costs, as well as the provision of employment opportunities.   The appropriate principle here would be to raise
the level of welfare for the handicapped to the mean
average, so far as this is possible through public
policy.   I further assume that where there is a degree
of risk attached to these services, as there will be
mortality risks attached to medical services for example,
that the level of risk for the handicapped should be
the same as that for the rest of the population, again
so far as this is practicable for public policy.

Note that the above interpretation of the equality
principle provides a distinct aim from the view that
society ought simply to satisfy minimum needs.   The
assumption behind this minimalist thesis is that it is
possible to isolate a minimum level of welfare below
which people ought not to fall. (7)   However, it has
always proved impossible to isolate a satisfactory
minimum standard for services provided in kind.   Neither
does the minimalist thesis provide any guidance on
distributive questions above the minimum.   By contrast,
the principle of equality represents an agreement to
share health risks by accepting the equal distribution
of the risks of unsatisfied need, or the shared costs of
compensation for the permanently handicapped.   With the
level of health services provided by the community's
political process, we can give sense to the concept of
the 'optimum health treatment', which can be interpreted
as the most efficient treatment given the resources that
society has decided to allocate towards the satisfaction
of medical needs.   In this way, the principles of equal
access or equal risks of unsatisfied need provide a
determinate meaning to the principle of equal welfare,
where needs are so large in relation to resources that
they could not all be satisfied.

4   CONSENT, RISK AND NEED

The approach outlined above, under which people
consent through the political process to a specified
level of morbidity and mortality risks, solves some
problems which have been raised concerning the correct
extent of medical redistribution.   For example, Fried
(1970, p. 201) conjectures that a full pooling of risks
might entail people being compelled to contribute
bodily organs, like kidneys, to an organ-bank on a
random basis, where this would not be harmful to the
donor and where it would benefit the recipient by

reducing the risk of mortality. In this type of example the risk-pool seems to entail moral obligations which are intuitively unacceptable. Is there any way of dealing with this dilemma if we accept some form of the principle of distribution according to need?

One obvious way in which the problem might be overcome, within the terms of the present theory, is to rely upon the distinction between natural capacities and the benefits which accrue to them. I have already argued that the egalitarian is only interested in maintaining claims on benefits, and not on the natural capacities which give rise to them, and it could be argued in the present case that compulsory kidney donations constituted a redistribution of natural capacities and not of benefits. This seems a weak argument however. What is actually redistributed by kidney transplants is the benefit of reduced mortality risks, to which the transplant of the bodily organ is a means, not an end itself. Moreover, the assumption is that the operation on the donor is neither fatal in itself nor does it increase his own mortality risks. To that extent it does not represent a diminution either of the donor's natural capacities or of the benefits which he derives from them. On this assumption the only disadvantage the donor suffers is the inconvenience of the operation itself, and this seems a small cost by comparison with the benefit which accrues to the recipient. The exchange appears optimal, in the sense that the recipient could compensate the donor for the inconvenience and still remain better off than he was before the transplant. Since at least one person gains, and nobody loses, it becomes difficult to see *exactly* what the ethical difficulty is meant to be.

The problem of perceiving the exact ethical difficulty arises once we have looked at the problem within the perspective of a time-slice theory of distribution. (8) A time-slice theory judges peoples' entitlements to welfare on the basis on the current distribution of benefit, and it will reallocate benefits accordingly. From the viewpoint of such a theory it is natural to think that the welfare claims of the potential recipient of the kidney donation are stronger than the claims of the selected donor, whoever he may be. There are two reasons for this. First, within a time-slice theory, unsatisfied needs always seem to create an entitlement to benefit, and hence an obligation upon others to meet the need. Second, the distribution of risks is based on a comparison between a person known to have a fatal disease and the rest of the population.

Given this basis for comparison, it is natural to suppose
that redistribution should take place in order to even
up the risks involved, once we accept the principle of
pooled risks.

The contract theory of justice, however, is not a
current time-slice theory, and so neither of these
conclusions follow. Under the hypothetical contract
members of the same society agree to share the
inequalities of advantage which follow upon the natural
distribution of abilities, but they do not agree to
cover all cases of need which arise as instances of
the inequality of natural advantage. Instead a situation
of equal welfare is defined as one in which there is an
equally distributed risk of unsatisfied need, where the
appropriated degree of risk is socially determined and
agreed. The right to benefit from the risk-pool does
not simply follow from the fact that one has needs, but
has also to be decided on the basis of whether people
have accepted a specified level of risk. Each person
in a society must ask himself whether the costs of a
kidney-bank scheme are worth having the assured benefits
of a transplant should he be in need of one in the case
of possible renal failure. If the benefits outweigh
the costs, then it would be rational to support setting
the level of risk lower than if he feels the costs
outweigh the benefits. Within the contract theory,
therefore, there is no *a priori* answer to the question
of whether it would be right to make the compulsory
transplant. The situation can only be decided by
discovering whether or not there has been social
agreement to cover this particular case of need, by
people consenting to be donors on a random basis, on the
understanding that they would be beneficiaries should
the need arise. The question can only be looked at by
examining the rights and obligations which are created
by people participating in a set of institutional
practices.

One important consequence of this approach is that
the *degree* of need is not at all decisive in determining
whether or not the transplant ought to be made. People
may consent to an equal distribution of risks, where
the level of risk is high or low. If they accept the
benefits of a high-risk system, for example by rejecting
a system under which they would be liable randomly to
supply bodily organs, then it may well be that serious
cases of need will arise. The seriousness of the cases,
however, will be no reason for making the transplants
outside of an explicit agreement to a donor system.
The contract theory allows a distinction to be made

between the degree of risk that people run, and the distribution of those risks: what matters from the viewpoint of justice is the distribution of risks.

In making the decision on whether to enter a system of risk-pooling which involves the possibility of random donations, the citizen only has to judge on the basis of the cost and benefits to himself. He is not asked to identify himself with the person suffering from renal failure, and determine what ought to be the extent of medical redistribution should he turn out to be in need. There is no obligation upon him therefore to prescribe distributive principles for hypothetical role-reversed situations as though they were actual. Hypothetical role-reversals presuppose that it is possible to come to an agreement on distributive questions, independently of the actual institutional rights and obligations which people set up by their consent. But since consent is regarded as the basis of the relevant entitlements, role-reversals will not help in determining the appropriate principles which are only discovered by examining what people have actually decided.

It may be argued that the predisposition to renal failure is not distributed randomly in the population, so that any scheme based upon consent will provide an incentive for the more healthily disposed members of the population to opt out of the system, thus weakening the communal basis of the risk-pool. However, there is no reason to think that this is a serious problem, since even if the actual predisposition towards renal failure (or other malfunctioning) is not randomly distributed, it will be extremely difficult for people to know their own individual chances of malfunctioning. They will have to base their decision, therefore, on aggregate statistical data concerning the likelihood of bodily malfunction among the population at large.

There is, of course, no reason in principle why schemes of mutual risk protection should always be society-wide. Society might decide, through the political process, that the costs of a particular risk-pool scheme are too high for the benefits it gave. However, a minority of people might decide the reverse, and it would be possible for them to enter into an agreement with one another to supply bodily organs on an appropriate basis in cases of individual malfunctioning. Conversely, a society which opted for compulsory redistribution could exempt a minority of its members from participation in the scheme provided they were prepared to forego their entitlements. Voluntary agreements of this sort to alter one's level of health risk need not be taken to violate the equal-risks principle. Rather the principle is applied among reference groups which are not identical with society at large. (9)

The requirement that risk-pool schemes involving organ transplants be based in a system of mutual insurance underlies the explanation for the apparent intuitive ethical difference between compulsory kidney transplants and compulsory blood donations. Fried (1970) himself admits that he is attracted to the latter but not the former (a response I share). One tempting basis for this distinction is to say that kidney transplants are potentially more damaging to the donor than are blood donations, so that it is simply a matter of the relative disadvantages of the two cases. However, this distinction does not fit the assumption which is made in the original supposition, namely that the random kidney donation is non-fatal and does not increase mortality risks. (Or if it does increase mortality risks, we can suppose in the present case that it does not increase them above the risks associated with blood donation.) Hence *this* distinction cannot be the basis for the apparent ethical difference.

The difference arises, I suggest, from the fact that most people in a society expect or feel entitled to blood transfusion should the need arise, whereas they do not feel an entitlement to kidney transplants. However, if people do feel a right to benefit from such a system, it seems natural to ask whether there should not be a corresponding obligation upon them to contribute towards the maintenance of the system, and whether there should not also be a method for enforcing the obligation should people fail to fulfil it. In the present context the problem is not to decide whether it is right to enforce such an obligation, but what accounts for the apparent ethical difference between the blood transfusion and kidney-transplant cases. If this explanation is valid, it suggests the essential correctness of basing entitlements to benefit from organ transplants on the historic rights which people acquire in a social institution by agreeing to accept the reciprocal obligations which that system imposes.

The good which is distributed under risk-pool mutual-aid schemes is the right to benefit in cases of need. However, if the right is dependent for its force on the acceptance of a particular set of obligations, then the justification for meeting the right in any specific case will be retrospective, based on the

undertakings which people have actually bound themselves
to. Satisfying the right, then, need not be justified
by the general utilitarian obligation of benevolence,
under which people are bound to relieve suffering. By
opting out of their obligations under the system of
mutual benefit people forfeit any rights they might have
in justice to the relevant goods which would satisfy
their needs. Of course there may be utilitarian
reasons for meeting their needs, but in such a case
there is no *obligation* upon other persons to provide
the appropriate benefits. It would be an act of
supererogation, not an obligation discharged from
considerations of justice. In this sense, the equal
right to benefit from specific mutual-aid schemes is
founded upon the prior principle of fairness, under
which people who conduct any joint enterprise according
to rules, which thus restrict their liberty, have a right
to similar submission from those who have benefited
by their actions (Hart, 1955, p. 61).

Such mutual-aid schemes only arise, however, within
the context of a general social commitment to reduce the
level of unsatisfied need, and are of concern simply to
those minority groups who are dissatisfied with the
level of risk acceptable to the majority of their
community. Although the principle of fairness provides
the basis for ascribing rights to benefit among such
groups, it cannot be made the reason for providing
general medical facilities, otherwise those individuals
who by natural endowment had few advantages to bring to
the mutual aid scheme, like the physically handicapped,
might have no right to benefit. The general justification
of medical facilities therefore has to remain couched
in terms of the justice of the equal welfare principle.

6

Institutions (1)

1 INTRODUCTION

In earlier chapters I have discussed some institutional
problems, relevant to the analysis of equality and its
justification. However, I have previously taken institutional problems as *examples* of points that I have
wanted to make about equality. Now I should like to
look at some of the institutional *implications* of the
argument I have advanced in earlier chapters. In this
chapter I shall take three specific areas of social
policy - health services, education and housing - and
bring out the conditions that the egalitarian would
wish to impose on their institutional form. In the
next chapter I shall consider some more general points
concerning social policy institutions and their role in
establishing and maintaining equality.
   This focus upon the general institution structure of
social policy is deliberate. Not only is equality of
economic welfare a difficult aim to achieve, it is
similarly difficult for the state to determine an equal
distribution of primary goods. Policies to achieve
equal resource allocation for publicly funded goods
run into the familiar problems of output measurement
and the impossibility of isolating the effects of any
one service. Nevertheless, although the performance of
particular services on the equality criterion may be
contested or impossible to measure, it should be
possible to decide what is a suitable egalitarian
structure of service provision. Answering this question
will certainly involve considerations of how easy it is,
within alternative administrative arrangements, to
equalise service provision, so that discussion of basic
institutional questions will have to take into account
the potential for equalisation with different

administrative systems. Nevertheless, it remains
easier to decide whether a particular institution has
the potential to equalise resources than it is to
determine how well the institution is actually performing
on the equality criterion.

Two further reasons lie behind the focus on
institutions. Institutional problems are discussed in
order to show that the principle of equality does not
always imply collectivism with respect to social
policy. Collectivism exists when there is not only
public funding of certain services, but also public
provision of a wide range of facilities. In discussing
three particular areas of policy I aim to show that,
though collectivist provision is justified in some cases,
there need be no general presumption in favour of
publicly provided services, as long as certain safe-
guards are enforced. The three services I shall be
discussing in this chapter are different in character,
and it would be a mistake to think that there is one
particular type of institutional framework which is a
model for all. By concentrating upon the institutional
implications of equality in each case, it is possible to
bring out the distinction between collectivism and
egalitarianism. Moreover, it is also possible to gain
a greater level of generality in the discussion if the
focus is upon the institutional forms of service implied
by equality rather than upon details of day-to-day
planning, which are inevitably connected with short and
medium term policy constraints.

2 HEALTH CARE

In the previous chapter I discussed the relevant
principles for distributing a service like health care
based on a conception of need. However, the principle
of distributing equally the risks of unsatisfied need
provides no guidance in itself to the institutional
form which health services should take. There may be
a variety of ways in which the principle might be
satisfied. Within existing systems of health care
delivery there are, for example, alternative means of
reducing morbidity and mortality. Preventive measures
may be substituted for curative facilities, sometimes
providing more efficient methods of reducing risks.

In discussing the appropriate institutions for health
care, I shall assume that the public authorities strike
a suitable balance between prevention and cure, and
will concentrate upon the problem of distribution as it

affects the latter. I shall maintain that any egalitarian system of curative provision will have the
following three features. It will be:
  (a)   free of charge for all but minor services;
  (b)   financed from progressive income taxation or
        expenditure taxes;
  (c)   show no marked regional or other social variations
        in the quality and quantity of service.
Clearly one institutional system which could satisfy
these criteria is the NHS and it may be contrasted with
a market system of private medical provision, in which
individuals insure themselves against illness out of
their own incomes and in which there would be geographical
and social variations in service quality depending upon
the purchasing power of local populations.

   The main argument in favour of NHS-style provision
is that it is a fairly efficient method of implementing
the principle of equal levels of benefit, to reduce
risks proportionate to need. By contrast, within a
perfectly competitive private market for health care
there ought to be as much discrimination in premiums
for risk as possible. In a competitive market individuals
with poor health prospects, whether through their own
fault or not, would face higher premiums than the
average, or a lower quality health care for the same
price. The system of private insurance against risk
has the unfortunate effect, therefore, of compounding
the natural inequalities of bodily condition with the
inequalities of cost implied by the actuarial financing
of market health services. The provision of health
care in kind under the NHS is one method by which
individuals can be compensated for natural inequalities
of bodily condition, and is thus a way of reducing
medical risks proportionate to need.

   It might be argued that an NHS system will overcome
the problem of compounding two sets of inequalities as
happens in a market system, but that it is not the
only means for achieving this end. There is no direct
move from competitive market provision to a state
provided system. Under a market system in any case
there is a tendency towards the pooling of risks because
of the effects of uncertainty (Arrow, 1963b, p. 33).
Hence we could still have private insurance provision, a
compulsory system of equal premiums, and the private
ownership of hospitals and other medical resources. In
principle such a system does not look so very different
from the NHS, and it is a little difficult to see what
could be said against it in terms of equality.
Nevertheless, even here, there are problems. Arrow (1971)

commenting on ·Titmuss's (1970) finding that the private
American health system was less efficient in some
respects than the British system, noted that this might
be due as much to the decentralised nature of the system
as to its private character. Nonetheless, it remains
true that it is easier to obtain the benefits of
centralisation under the NHS scheme than it is for a
private system, simply because the private system is
independent and retains the power to resist state
intervention. (1) By contrast a centralised administrative
structure makes it easier to cope with variations in
health care which arise through regional cost differences.
A compulsory system of equal premiums would be insufficient
to provide equal levels of care, since the costs of
provisions might be higher in some regions than others,
e.g., to compensate doctors for moving into unattractive
areas. Private insurance would require a complicated
system of subsidies and cash transfers to iron out such
cost discrepancies. (2)

Of course, alternative administrative arrangements
not involving NHS-style provision can be imagined for
transferring health resources. For example, tax-
supported subsidies to the poor combined with rationing
on the rich might in principle provide equality in the
consumption of health care. The difficulty here is that
health care subsidies should not only be linked inversely
to income, but they also should be differentiated
according to the degree of medical need on the part of
each individual. But the complications of providing cash
subsidies in proportion to need are enormous, and there
would be almost insurmountable complexity in identifying
those clinical states which entitled persons to an extra
subsidy. Administratively it would be simpler to provide
the service, thus producing a direct link-up between the
need and the benefit that is provided. For this reason,
the NHS may be the most appropriate 'second best' solution
available for the problem of distributing health care
(Lindsay, 1969, p. 87). A further advantage of an NHS
system is that it is financed either out of progressive
income taxes or from expenditure taxes on consumption,
and not by a system of equal flat-rate premiums. In
terms of the social contract theory of justice which I
have been developing, this type of financing can be
regarded as the expression of a willingness on the part
of all citizens to pool not only the unequally distributed
benefits of clinical states, but also the full range of
benefits which accrue from the natural distribution of
talents and abilities.

Given the strengths of the NHS in pooling risks and

in administratively providing a link between resources
and the satisfaction of needs, what further difficulties
are there in favouring that sort of provision as against
the private market? Perhaps the strongest arguments
against the NHS system have been offered by Buchanan
(1965) who sees an inconsistency between the behaviour
appropriate to the supply of health services and the
rational behaviour of a consumer in a free system:

> Governments that are broadly democratic can be
> successful in providing 'free' services but only
> if they do so within institutions that promote
> general consistency in the social decision-making
> process. In models that approximate to the
> British structure . . . in their *private or individual
> choice* behaviour as potential users or demanders of
> health-medical treatment, individuals are inconsistent
> with their *public or collective choice* behaviour
> as vote-taxpayers who make decisions on supplying
> these same services. (p. 4)

The specific form the inconsistency takes can be
expressed as follows. There is a contrast between
decisions appropriate to demand behaviour and decisions
appropriate to supply behaviour in a system like the NHS.
On the demand side we have the straightforward principle
that where demand is at all elastic consumers will
increase their demand as prices tend to zero. On the
supply side by contrast, expenditure cannot rise in order
to meet the increased demand, because decisions on
resource allocation will be made on an opportunity cost
basis. Consequently there will be a short-fall of
expenditure relative to demand because the policy of
zero-pricing leads to excessive demand relative to the
resources which, on opportunity costs grounds, it makes
sense to spend on health care. On the basis of this
simple antinomy Buchanan aims to explain the under-
capitalisation of the health service, and the other
features indicating lack of resources.

This analysis of the NHS is based on a series of
deductions from the theoretical postulates of micro-
economic decision-making, and stands in need of empirical
corroboration. In particular it is important to have
some evidence on the elasticity of demand for health care,
since Buchanan's argument crucially rests on such
elasticity being present in the system. The only
evidence cited in support of the view that elasticity
of demand is sufficient to increase consumption is the
rise in dispensed prescriptions on the abolition of
charges. Some of this rise is of course explained by an
increase in certified sickness over the same period, and

some of it to an increased willingness on the part of
doctors to prescribe drugs when they know patients
do not have to pay. Some, no doubt, is due to an
increase in the consumption of health care, and,
strictly speaking, even the increased willingness of
doctors to prescribe drugs ought to be included in a
similar category, since from the point of view of
consumption increases it does not matter how they come
about on the abolition of charges, merely that they occur.
     However, prescriptions are only a relatively small,
if significant, part of the NHS bill. (3) In other
respects the behavioural model on which Buchanan relies
is less satisfactory in explaining patterns of use in
health services. For example, since the introduction
of the NHS in 1948 visits by people to their local GP
have *dropped* by 25 per cent or so (Klein, 1975, p. 93).
Nor has this fall in visits to GPs, amounting to
twenty-million visits per year, been compensated for
by an increase in people admitted to hospital outpatient
departments, where the number of admissions has only
risen by five million in the same period. These
figures are of course crude, because they do not, for
instance, take into account the changing nature of the
demand. But it is surely striking that during a period
when the population has risen by 10 per cent the demand
on the NHS should drop - in marked contrast to the
prediction we should expect from the axiom of an
economic model.
     A further difficulty with the model is that by far
and away the largest expenditure goes on hospitals and
their maintenance, where there are grounds for believing
that the elasticities of demand will be lower than the
elasticities for drugs. There are a number of reasons
for this. Being a hospital patient is by no means
costless, even when the price of treatment is set to
zero. The patient incurs loss of earnings from work as
well as the inconvenience and disruption due to the
interruption of normal routine. Moreover, it is much
more difficult to feign illness when it is a matter of
hospital care than when it is a matter of applying for
drugs. Indeed this link-up between needs and the service
meeting the need has already been stressed as one of
the principal administrative advantages of the NHS
system. For these reasons there is good ground for
saying that elasticity of demand for the major part of
health care will not be very great, and consumption
therefore will not be susceptible to variations in price.
If large prices are advocated as a method of overcoming
the problem of demand, then this sort of proposal

immediately runs into the problem that the pricing of
health care involves compounding the inequalities of
bodily condition.

There is, however, some independent evidence for
Buchanan's contention on the supply side that people in
general underestimate the cost of providing services
which are paid for out of the public purse. The policy
question is: should we favour a market-type solution
to this problem (Buchanan's reform essentially involves
limiting the amount of health care to which people will
be entitled under the NHS), or should we find some
other way of bringing the supply and demand decisions
into a closer relationship? This is obviously a large
and complex question which it is impossible adequately
to discuss here. However, if the present National
Insurance health contribution were made to cover more
of the costs of the NHS, with an appropriate off-set
against the general tax bill, then it would be possible
for people more clearly to see how much of their income
was going towards health care and thereby appreciate
the costs of providing the service. One reason for
advocating this reform is that the Government Social
Survey found that 60 per cent of the public considered
that the entire cost of the NHS was already met, not
from general taxes, but from the weekly National Insurance
contribution. Since the contribution in fact only
covers 8½ per cent of the cost, there is little wonder
that people think the NHS is a good bargain (Cooper,
1975, p. 83). Now that the old National Insurance
contribution has ceased to be a regressive flat-rate
payment and has become a proportionate Social Security
tax, there is no strong equity argument for keeping the
contribution as low as possible.

The most usual objection to this sort of proposal
is that it runs directly counter to the tradition in
British fiscal policy of not ear-marking taxes for
specific purposes. But there seems to be no more
rationale for this policy than for the Treasury's
general prejudice in favour of a single Consolidated
Fund for central government revenue as opposed to
distinct funds which separate redistributive from non-
redistributive public expenditure (cf. Brittan, 1969,
pp. 121-2). A more serious difficulty with financing
the whole of health service costs from the Social
Security tax is that the payments to the NHS from the
Consolidated Fund include tax revenues from indirect
and corporate sources. However, there migh be a case
for incurring the disadvantages of narrowing the
financial base of the NHS, if this led to greater

public awareness of the relevant social costs.
Indeed public discussion on the political implications
of government expenditure requires a greater distinction to be made among the different purposes to which
public expenditure is devoted. A democratic choice
on the level and quality of health care a society
should sustain is impossible unless it is clear to
people what the costs of such a service are.

3 EDUCATION

In part the rationale for extending the list of primary
social goods beyond income and wealth is to separate
the problem of their distribution from the general
problems of engineering a satisfactory income distribution. By this separation, important benefits are
isolated in order that they may be distributed equally,
or at least less unequally than the ability to pay for
them. This aspect of primary goods theory becomes
particularly significant in the case of education.
There are three reasons why education especially
should be included in the list of primary goods.
   (1) The unequal distribution of parental income
will affect the child's entitlement to educational
resources. This means that the benefit entitlements
of one person are influenced by the arbitrary circumstances of parental earnings' power.
   (2) Education is important for the individual
because it provides him with the means to other
benefits: in economic terms it is a form of investment
as well as consumption.
   (3) The distribution of educational resources may
have important consequences if ability is less unequally distributed than income. The benefits of an
equal distribution of educational resources will include,
in the long run, a less unequal distribution of income
by reducing the scarcity of those people able to
extract rent for talents in short supply, and
decreasing the number of unskilled persons in a
society.
   However, there is no general justification for
including all forms of education within the category of
primary goods, and there may be reasons, in justice,
why higher and advanced education should be excluded
from the staus of primary goods. Not to do so may lead
to inequitable results. For example, suppose that two
brothers are contemplating their future careers aged
eighteen or so. One wants to become an accountant and

the other wishes to open a shop. The effect of including
further education in the list of primary goods is to
provide the first with the investment resources to
carry through his plans, but not the second, who will
normally have to borrow money at the going rate of
interest in order to make the necessary investment.
There seems to be a *prima facie* argument therefore for
excluding higher education from the scope of distributive
considerations. However, in order to bring the present
discussion within manageable proportions, I shall leave
aside the complex problems of distributive justice
which arise in the financing of higher education, and
concentrate upon the distribution of education up to
secondary level, assuming it satisfies the requirements
of a benefit being a primary good.

The contractual theory of justice requires educational
benefits, as a primary good, to be distributed equally.
However, in practice there are severe problems in
stipulating what the application of equality would
amount to in this particular case. The relevant equality
may be defined as an equal opportunity for each child
to develop basic social and intellectual skills as
well as his own particular abilities and talents. But
this definition is open to various interpretations, both
in respect to what constitutes a relevant opportunity
and in respect of the level of cognitive and intellectual
ability used to judge whether the opportunity criterion
has been satisfied. Equal opportunities could simply be
defined in input terms, and measured by such indices as
per-pupil expenditures or staff/pupil ratios. However,
this is unlikely to be satisfactory as an adequate
measure of opportunity, since equality of expenditure
may not guarantee equality of educational resources:
for example, teachers may be more expensive to provide
in one area than in another, or inherited variations
in capital equipment may reduce the value of some
current expenditures and not others. As an alternative,
then, opportunities may be defined in output terms.
In this case, however, there is the problem of determining the appropriate level of output. Is output equal
when children of the *same* ability and background achieve
similar cognitive levels, or is it only equal when
children of *different* abilities and backgrounds achieve
similar levels of cognitive performance? (Coleman,
1968, p. 17.)

Under the first interpretation of the output
criterion variations in inputs will be allowed only to
cover such factors as variations in costs, but not to
compensate children for disadvantages of home background

or environmental influence. Under the second interpretation compensatory variations in input would be
allowed, e.g., to provide special language tuition to
those children who did not speak the native language of
their country of habitation. If the performance of the
education system is to be judged purely by reference to
considerations of justice, and not, for example, in
terms of the promotion of certain types of excellence,
then there is a good case for saying that the second and
stronger output criterion should be used. For presumably
by equalising so far as possible the cognitive abilities
of different people, their average lifetime welfare is
equalised as well. On the egalitarian theory of justice,
therefore, 'positive discrimination' as advocated by
Plowden (1967, p. 57) would be allowed. (4)

A major difficulty with notions of positive
discrimination or compensatory education is that much
of the available empirical evidence suggests that the
educational process can do little to change the aptitudes
and attainment levels which children bring with them to
the school. Jencks et al. (1973) have argued forcibly
that programmes of compensatory education in the USA have
had negligible impact both upon the cognitive performance
of children and upon their future occupational mobility.
The English evidence is more ambiguous, and some initial
successes have been claimed for the EPA experiments
(Gray, 1975; Halsey, 1972). At present, then, the
value of compensatory education is an open question.

The normative implications of these findings may be
considered with respect to two possibilities:
(a)   education may have virtually no impact upon
       cognitive ability, which will be determined by
       other factors;
(b)   education may raise cognitive ability, but at very
       large social cost.
If (a) is true, and education can do little to raise
cognitive ability, no matter what the level of educational
inputs is, then the egalitarian should fall back on the
weaker criterion of output, and judge the distribution
of resources by how far they preserve equality of
cognitive performance for children of the same ability,
home background, etc. By contrast, if (b) is true, and
it is possible but enormously expensive to compensate
children for background educational deficiencies, then
the appropriate rule would be to continue to spend
resources on improving education until that point at
which the consequent reduction in the inequality of
economic welfare was smaller than it would be if the
same amount of money were spent on other social

programmes or in other ways. In other words, the
marginal contribution to the reduction of inequality by
educational expenditure should not be smaller than any
alternative contributions to the same end by other
means.

It is perhaps natural to think that the best
institutions for promoting equality of educational
opportunity are state schools paid for directly out of
progressive taxation. However, this is not necessarily
so, and there have been suggestions for reforming the
state system and replacing it with a system of educational
vouchers. Under this scheme parents would be given
vouchers by the state which entitled them to buy so
much education (dependent on the value of the voucher)
at the school of their choice. The schools would be
able to charge what they liked, and they would be able
to redeem the vouchers by exchanging them at their face
value with the state. The supposed advantages of the
scheme are that it would increase parental freedom of
choice and the diversity of education provision. For
instance more progressive education might be provided
for more people if it was so desired, since any qualified
person would be entitled to supply educational services.
The question I want to raise in the present discussion
is whether the egalitarian could accept a voucher system
or not. This is clearly not the only question concerning the proposed reform, most obviously if it were
accepted it would create a number of administrative
difficulties. But it is pertinent for anyone who places
a high value on educational equality.

One difficulty with discussing vouchers as a possible
reform is that the proposal can be implemented in a
variety of ways. Indeed the system's flexibility has
been claimed as a major advantage by its proponents
(Maynard, 1975, p. 47). However, it does complicate
discussion on the merits of the proposal, particularly
if the suitability of the scheme is being judged from
its relevance to equality, since there are a number of
voucher schemes which would not be satisfactory on the
equality criterion. For example, under Friedman's
(1962, pp. 89-98) proposals, parents would be allowed
to supplement the value of the vouchers out of their
own income, and no special contribution would be made
towards the travelling costs of children of poor parents.
Since there is no evidence that the sellers of high
quality services move into poor and ghetto areas, there
is little reason to believe that the sellers of high
quality educational services would move into such
neighbourhoods. As Levin, (1968, p. 34) points out,

not only is there no Saks Fifth Avenue in Harlem, there
is no Macy's, Gimbels, Korvettes, or Kleins. Analogously
there are unlikely to be any Etons, Marlboroughs or
St Paul's in Bermondsey, under any system of education
which depends upon relative purchasing power. (5)

However, if the merits of the voucher system are to
be fairly assessed, then one should consider schemes
which are aimed explicitly at the promotion of greater
educational equality and improved services to the worst-
off members of the population. One such scheme is the
Jencks voucher. Under this proposal, implemented for
an experimental period in Alum Rock, California, parents
are given a voucher equal to the average cost of
schooling for each child, and a second 'compensatory'
voucher, inversely related to means, is issued to
families whose income is relatively low. All transport
costs are paid for the children who have to travel to
the school of their parents' choice. The schools are
legally obliged to provide a large amount of information
about themselves, and if the demand for places exceeds
the supply, then at least 50 per cent of the available
places have to be allocated in a random fashion.

The Jencks scheme has many of the advantages associated
with voucher schemes in general. It allows scope for
parental freedom of choice and for educational experimentation. It is also asserted that it is more efficient,
because the greater competitiveness of the educational
market should filter out less-successful schools: for
this reason it ought to be possible for the government
to finance improvements in the quality of education
without being out of pocket. (However, this theoretical
advantage may be counterbalanced by the increased transport costs borne by the state.) Moreover, it should
make parents more aware of the costs of providing
education. It also seems to contain a number of
features to protect the disadvantaged child, for example,
in the payment of transport costs.

One general problem with voucher schemes is said to
be the way in which they provide an incentive for
intelligent and articulate parents to cluster in a
minority of schools, and so weaken the pressure for
improvements in schools at large. There is certainly
evidence for example that parents who at present send
their children to school outside the state system take
less of an interest in state schools than they otherwise
would. (6) However, in this respect the Jencks scheme
seems to go as far as is practically possible in meeting
the problem. Both the allocation of places on a random
basis and the enforcement of minimum standards on all

schools in the market-place would have the effect of
counteracting this tendency. In any case the comparison
is not really between a voucher scheme in which articulate
parents are clustered, through choice, into a few schools
and a state scheme in which they are evenly spread
throughout all schools. It is between a voucher scheme
in which clustering through choice is regulated, and a
state system in which clustering occurs through the
choice which parents make of where to live. On this
second comparison it is not clear that the voucher
scheme comes out the worse.

One genuine problem with the Jencks scheme is more
intrinsic and important. This concerns the way in which
the value of vouchers is varied according to *income*.
Strictly speaking it would be preferable to have them
varied according to the relative *costs* to parents of
alternative schools and to the relative *needs* of their
children for such things as special reading instruction.
In other words the distribution of educational expenditure,
via vouchers, is unlikely to be linked-up with the
distribution of educational costs or needs.   The
significance of this latter point is brought out in
evidence on the functioning of EPA's. EPA's can in
some respects be regarded as an administrative version
of the compensatory aspects of the Jencks scheme, in
which the benefits are transferred in kind to poor
parents, rather than by the supplementation vouchers.
Extra resources are provided under the EPA system to
schools in neighbourhoods which are relatively deprived,
the object being to compensate the children of poor
parents, rather than by the supplementation of vouchers.
educational disadvantages are not co-incidental with low
incomes. Hence, although it is true that EPA schools
have a higher proportion of poor readers than schools
elsewhere, it is also true that about 75 per cent of
children in EPA schools are competent readers, while
there are plenty of poor readers outside these schools
(Barnes, 1974, pp. 12-13). The same expenditure might
be better employed in providing more remedial teachers
in all schools, rather than concentrating expenditure
in particular areas. Similarly, under a voucher system,
it would be preferable to supplement parental vouchers
not on the basis of income, but on the basis of the
child's educational performance. Just as poor readers
are not found exclusively in areas of general social
deprivation, so they are not found solely among poor
parents.

Similarly there is a case for varying the value of
vouchers not with income but with cost. Ghetto

schools are likely to be more expensive to run than
suburban schools. Teachers will be more expensive if
they are to be attracted in sufficient quantities, and
capital equipment may have a shorter life. But incomes
are not identical in ghetto areas. There is no reason
why comparatively well-off parents, who have to send
their children to the local school in a high cost area,
should be penalised relative to the poor parents who are
receiving supplementary vouchers and transport costs
to send their children to low-cost suburban schools.

Under a state-run educational system the distribution
of available resources may be varied in accordance
with considerations of cost and need by the discretion
of administrators and officials. The value of compensatory vouchers cannot be varied in similar ways. Thus,
the current EPA system could be changed into a method
for channelling resources to educationally-deprived
pupil groups, rather than to schools, whereas there is
no comparable reform that could be made in the case of
vouchers. The difficulty, of course, is that the
advantages of the state system in this respect are
bought at the cost of a loss of diversity and variation
in the school system. However, as with the argument on
the clustering of articulate parents, it is important
to avoid 'nirvana' comparisons: that is, comparing the
advantages of a smoothly functioning state system with
the disadvantages of alternative proposals. Although
the existing state system may provide an institutional
framework in which expenditure can be matched to costs
and needs, there may be factors which in practice
prevent it from successfully performing this matching.

Moreover, in the present state of our knowledge, we
lack sufficient evidence in crucial areas to decide for
or against the introduction of vouchers. For instance
it would be useful to have more evidence on the extent
to which the school can compensate for environmentally-
determined educational deficiencies. If it were true
that schools can do something to compensate, then this
would count against the voucher scheme, because it
lacks the link-up between educational needs and resources
which it is possible to provide in the state system.
On the other hand, if school performance were effectively
determined by home, genes and environment, then the
most that one could hope for educational provision would
be that it guaranteed equal access to the available
resources, even if those resources could not be used to
compensate people for educational deficiencies. The
case for vouchers in these circumstances would be strong
since they would bring a number of important benefits

to the educational system - diversity, decentralisation and flexibility - which are absent from the present system, without incurring any disadvantages. Working out the balance of advantages then between the present system and the proposals for reform requires more evidence. To say this, however, at least suggests that the egalitarian should favour experimentation with the voucher scheme to see how it would perform in practice, and that there is no reason why he should reject in principle the voucher proposals.

4 HOUSING

Until this point in the chapter the benefits whose institutional form I have been discussing could be classified as primary goods in the full sense. The possession of these benefits was essential in maintaining people at a certain level of welfare, even though income might be equally distributed. The problem in each case was to decide the appropriate institutional form of the equal benefits principle. With housing the problem is somewhat different.

For various reasons housing cannot be regarded as a primary good like any other. Rather than being a necessary condition for achieving similar levels of welfare on the same income, housing consumption can be regarded as one way in which people experience their welfare entitlements. Two people on the same income may live in quite different housing, but this need not imply that they experience unequal levels of welfare: they may be mixing their consumption bundles in different ways because they have different tastes and preferences. Variations of taste and preference thus make it undesirable to supply housing in the same manner as health services or education. Any social policy measures on housing ought to recognise the role of free choice in housing consumption. Why not, then, simply leave the supply of housing to the free market, instead of looking on housing as a matter of social services policy at all? There are, I think, five answers to this question:

(1) Housing is still in some sense a primary good, since it provides the necessary condition for people to do whatever they want to do.

(2) Housing consumption may involve certain social costs which, in the absence of government intervention, can work to the serious detriment of other members of the community. The most obvious example here are public

health risks, and much housing legislation has its
origin in a concern for the dangers to public health
from unregulated or poor housing.

(3)   The supply of housing is relatively inelastic
under normal market conditions (hence the sudden price
changes in the housing market). Replacing
poor quality housing stock would therefore take a long
time if simply left to the market (cf. Tobin, 1970,
p. 462).

(4)   The building of houses has an investment aspect.
Housing is largely a 'second-hand' market, and <u>the
houses which are built today will still be on the
market for future generations for many years hence.
Any concern for the welfare of future generations in this
respect is likely to involve higher costs to consumers
now in order to build houses to a standard suitable for
future purchasers.</u>

(5)   In a system in which incomes are inequitably
distributed, there may be special reasons for protecting
some types of consumption, in which housing could be
included because of its primary goods aspect.

These reasons make it important to introduce a social
services aspect into the regulation of the housing
market, and provide the rationale for subsidies to
particular tenant groups. For instance, if the government imposes certain minimum standards on houses for
public health or investment reasons this raises the cost
of housing to low-income purchasers, who may then require
a subsidy.

When deciding on the institutional structure of
housing from the social policy angle, it is important
therefore to bear in mind the special circumstances of
housing as discussed above. However, proposals for the
reform of housing policy are further complicated by the

complexity of current housing subsidies, distributed in
an arbitrary and inefficient way. Indeed the complexity
of the current institutional arrangements, already
touched upon in chapter 2, creates one reason for
reform, since they are a cause of a great deal of mal-
distribution in the spread of housing subsidies. Moreover, the present structure of subsidies creates problems
of reforming other social policy programmes. It would
be impossible, for example, to introduce a fair negative
income tax or social dividend scheme unless the
current structure of housing subsidies were reformed.
At present means-tested social security benefits include
a special allowance for housing in order to overcome
the problem of regional variations in rent levels,
which do not simply reflect variations in social cost

but arbitrary judgments by local authorities concerning
the 'proper' level of rents.

For the egalitarian the proper aim of the housing
policy should be to ensure an adequate supply of housing
to meet demands, and to subsidise low-income households
in meeting their housing needs. For this reason the
policy of subsidising certain types of housing stock,
as is now done through subsidised rents to council
tenants and subsidised mortgages to house purchasers,
seems mistaken. There is no link-up under this sort of
arrangement between housing consumption and the ability
to pay. It would be preferable to have a single cash
housing subsidy allowance which varied inversely with
income, and which resembled the present income tax
allowance for house purchasers on their mortgage interest
repayments (cf. Klein et al., 1974, p. 56). The
incidental advantages of such a subsidy would be to end
two particular anomalies, namely the subsidy to the
richer council tenants through an artificially low rent,
and the subsidy to those wealthy owner occupiers who
continue to gain tax exemption on the interest component
of their mortgage repayment. In neither case would the
low income earners in each tenure group suffer from the
change of policy, since the special subsidy they received
could be designed to cover any increased costs they would
pay under these other policy changes.

Housing is an area where there are distinct advantages
in operating through the tax system. Already the
system is used to subsidise those who have mortgage
interest repayments, and most other people, who were to
be subsidised in the same way, would not be brought for
the first time into the tax system. The Inland Revenue
would have to process the extra demand of retired people
who claimed a subsidy on their rent, but to some extent
the extra manpower could be supplied by the Supplementary
Benefits Commission who would no longer have the separate
task of calculating housing needs and resources. (7)
Paying cash subsidies, rather than providing housing in
kind, has the twin merits of concentrating help where
it is most needed, i.e., low income groups, and increasing many people's freedom of choice as to whether they
want to rent or buy. Moreover, tenants in privately-
rented accommodation would benefit, since the allowance
would have none of the stigma and information costs
attached to the present system of rent allowances.

None of this need imply that the role of local
authorities in providing housing should be reduced.
Councils could still build houses to rent or buy, and
they could be encouraged to build special types of

accommodation for particular social groups, e.g., single-parent families. Moreover, because housing supply is relatively inelastic, councils may have a special role to play in overcoming the hiccups of the housing market, by building for periods of housing shortage and easing their building during the periods of boom. But their role in this respect would be pragmatically determined. There is certainly no reason in principle why the egalitarian should be committed to the public ownership of housing. The principle of equal welfare requires an equal apportionment of private benefits among citizens. Communal ownership of primary goods is not required by this principle. If communal ownership is to be justified as intrinsically desirable, then it will be on grounds other than those of strict equality.

5   EXEMPTION FROM COLLECTIVELY SUPPLIED BENEFITS

In this chapter I have argued for the collective supply of health services, and discussed alternative educational systems which, in both cases, would tie the beneficiary to the consumption of certain benefits. In both these cases, even with educational vouchers, there is a strong element of collective supply in the provision of the benefits. What rights, under this system, should people have to exempt themselves from being beneficiaries of the system, and enjoy a reduction in their tax bill?

When discussing the limits of compensatory transfers (chapter 4.2) I argued against the paternalistic case that people should have no right of exemption and compensation in those cases where they consumed benefits financed by themselves. However, it was implicitly assumed in that discussion that the people involved would not be spending the cash taken as compensation on social-welfare goods, but on something else. In the present section I shall drop this assumption, and take instead the case where people do not use the publicly-provided health or educational systems, but wish to purchase their own supply of these goods on the private market. I shall also drop the assumption that the background distribution of income accords with the relevant principle of equality. The question, then, becomes whether people who prefer private health or educational provision to public provision should be exempted from the costs which they would have made on the public system, and allowed an appropriate tax reduction.

There appears to be a strong equity argument for
saying that they should be exempted. *Ex hypothesi* they
are contributing to any redistribution that might be
licensed by the principles of justice, and they are
merely claiming exemptions from the payment of charges
for a service from which they do not benefit. Moreover,
in the present case, the paternalist argument is
irrelevant, since those in question are intending to
consume some kind of social policy benefit; they merely
prefer private supply to public provision. What, then,
are the arguments for saying that they should not be
exempted?

There are two possible answers to this question, both
of which rely on the (surely uncontentious) premise
that in not exempting people from the costs of the
service one is providing them with an incentive to use
the public system. The first argument is that in
providing an incentive for people to remain in the public
system, one is fostering a better type of social
relationship than otherwise. For example, one frequent
justification for common schooling is that this produces
a 'social mix', which would not be so likely under a
system in which some people were given an incentive to
use private educational provision. Within a common
school environment, it is assumed that children will
learn to understand the viewpoint of one another, coming
thereby to acquire a sense of self-respect and respect
for others. Barry (1965, p. 122) dubs the underlying
value of this argument 'integration', and classifies it
as one ideal-regarding form of the equality principle.
In terms of the contractarian theory of justice we may
say that the social mix argument assumes common
facilities will create equality of status or esteem, and
this consequence is a benefit which should be traded-off
against the equity of exempting people from charges for
a service they do not use.

Being a consequentialist argument, this proposal is
directly susceptible to empirical refutation, and indeed
there is some evidence to show that one of its premises
is not always valid. Common educational facilities may
not have the effect of increasing a person's sense of
self-respect, even as a child. Thus, a number of
radical community groups in the USA run separate
pre-schools for black children, with the specific
intention of providing an environment in which children
can develop a consciousness of racial pride. The
separateness of the school is explicitly regarded as a
method for counteracting prejudicial attitudes in
society at large. If there is no reason, in principle,

therefore, for favouring common schools in all circumstances, the proponent of the view that non-users of
state services should be exempt payment will have to
withdraw his assertion that social mix considerations
ought always to outweigh equity considerations.
Moreover, in order properly to assess the benefits of
the trade-off between equity and the social mix, one
would need positive empirical evidence that common
schooling had the effects that were intended.

Although a possible line of counter-attack, therefore,
the social-mix argument may seem relatively weak in
some circumstances against equity considerations.
Another counter-argument of a different style is that
to exempt non-users from tax will lower the standards of
the public services by encouraging a greater demand for
scarce resources outside the state system. For example,
to exempt people from a proportion of their NHS charge
would allow them to spend that sum, suitably supplemented, on private medical facilities, and the result
might be to draw off doctors from the NHS into full-
time private practice. Similarly, teachers may move
from state education into the private sector if the
latter were encouraged to grow by parents being exempt
a portion of their tax. The result of this process
would be to lower standards for those who were dependent
wholly on the state service, either by causing a
direct shortage of manpower resources, or by raising
the costs of supplying the same service under increased
competition from the private sector.

In essence, this appears to be a strong argument and
is, I think, decisive against the equity considerations
provided that certain circumstances obtain. Thus, to
be valid, the argument's assumption must be true that
an improved private sector would be in direct competition
with the public sector for scarce resources. It may be
that some people would not teach at all unless they
could work in a private school, so that an improved
private sector may draw resources into education that
would not otherwise be available, and the same may also
be true in the medical field. Moreover, the assumption
is also made that there will be a sufficient number of
people claiming a tax exemption to create a significant
increase in demand for private services. If this is not
true, there will be little substance in the argument that
the increase in private provision will be deleterious
with respect to the public system.

It is sometimes assumed that a vigorous private sector
in health and education is not harmful to the public
sector in any case, since its better quality provision

pioneers the way for improvements in public facilities. However, this argument would only be successful (assuming its empirical premise to be true) by ignoring entitlements based on considerations of justice. Even if a vigorous private sector did succeed in raising average levels of service in some fields, this would not be a decisive consideration unless one believed that the maximisation of average utility should always be preferred to a just distribution of available resources. Moreover, the argument seems to presuppose that permanent inequalities of provision in health and education will be necessary if average standards are to rise at a fast enough rate. Given this supposition, there may well be a reason for saying that an equal distribution of resources should be preferred to an unequal one, in those circumstances where unequal provision does not promise subsequent equality at a higher level of well-being.

I conclude, therefore, that there are reasons for not exempting those who do not benefit from a service from the appropriate charge, when circumstances suggest that the consequence of this policy would be to lower standards of public provision.

7   Institutions (2)

1 GENERAL FRAMEWORK OF SOCIAL POLICY

In the previous chapter I discussed some specific
institutional questions raised by the application of the
equality principle to areas of social policy. In this
chapter I shall discuss some of the more general
questions which have been raised concerning the state's
role in promoting an equal distribution of social welfare
benefits. However, before passing on to these questions,
it is first necessary to say something about the overall
institutional framework within which social policies are
set, since assumptions concerning this framework will
affect the subsequent discussion.
   I shall assume that the promotion of economic
equality does not involve abandoning the competitive
market economy as the principal method of production and
exchange. As far as the promotion of economic welfare
is concerned public policy may be divided into two main
categories: the task of allocating productive resources
efficiently; and the task of distributing the benefits
of social co-operation according to some rule of justice.
By maintaining a market framework the government accepts
the distinction between the problems of allocation and
distribution, with the efficient allocation of resources
left to the market and the just distribution of resources
determined by an appropriate system of transfers. (1)
   Naturally the effect of the market is to base the
original distribution of income upon the marginal
contribution which people make to the social product -
to labour output that is - rather than basing it on
considerations of welfare. For this reason it might be
tempting to argue that any concern for the equalisation
of economic welfare required the abolition of the market
system. However, the problem arises not from the nature

of the market and its working but from a more general
concern with efficiency. An efficient centrally-
planned, non-market economy will reward individuals
differently depending upon their effort, acquired assets
and abilities (Bergson, 1966, pp. 183-4). Inequality in
the original distribution is not solely confined to
market economies, therefore, but will arise in any system
of production which is concerned with producing the
maximum output for the least cost in line with consumer
preferences. A particular difficulty which arises in
this respect is that no economic system can distinguish
between differential wages which are paid to compensate
for disutility and differentials which arise because
individuals can extract rent for scarce talents and
abilities. (2) Any viable economic system will find
it impossible in practical terms to tax incentives$_2$
without at the same time taxing incentives$_1$. This
fact may provide a special justification for state
educational transfers, as well as a more general system
of transfers based on welfare considerations, since the
more the educational system increases the supply of
scarce talents and skills the more equal will be the
corresponding distribution of economic welfare.

The task of improving and equalising the distribution
of welfare falls therefore not to the economic system
but to the political process. In particular I assume
that in a just society the state will make transfer
payments to specific categories of people, as well as
provide the particular services discussed in the previous
chapter. These transfer payments will be used to
benefit the unemployed, the sick and the old in particular,
alongside a system of family allowances to cover the costs
of children.

Having assumed that a just society would make transfers
in kind of the type discussed in the previous chapter,
I do not suggest that the examples of the previous
chapter were exhaustive - some transport subsidies might
be justifiable on distributive grounds for instance -
but it should be stressed that the form of state commitment is not identical for all cases. For example,
although there seem to be good pragmatic reasons for
state medical provision, in the case of education the
state may only finance the benefit rather than provide
it in kind. The principle of equality will be relevant
to deciding what form these services should take, but
it is impossible to use the principle *a priori* to
stipulate that state provision is always desirable.

One particular reason for providing these specific
services in kind may also be mentioned. The provision

of equal access to certain specific services is easier
to engineer than a fair income distribution, since the
latter would need to be assessed not simply by reference
to a reduction in income inequality, however measured,
but more especially by reference to a reduction in
welfare inequalities. As we have seen, no practicable
and efficient economy provides the means for bringing
about this end to any satisfactory degree. In practice,
income differentials will remain, only some of which
could be justified by reference to the principle of
compensating for disutility. Protecting equality of
access to a specific range of primary goods is the only
way of overcoming this problem.

At this point, however, a problem of justification
arises. How does the state acquire the right to enforce
a particular distribution of welfare? This is a
particular problem for the interpretation of social
contract theory which I offered, since under that
interpretation there need be no legitimate inference
from the statement 'Social state X is just' to the
statement 'Society should promote social state X'.
Simply by virtue of the fact that the hypothetical contracting parties choose a particular distribution of
welfare as just, it is not always possible to justify
the means which may be necessary to promote that
distribution.

Indeed, it is not inconsistent to ask: should the
state promote a supposedly just distribution of welfare?
To raise the question may seem contradictory, since
justice is an end in itself, which requires no further
argument for its promotion. Yet there are just states
of affairs which the state may have no place in
promoting, because of the intrinsic impracticality of
its acting in the appropriate way. For example, a
just society with respect to social status will be one
in which people enjoy equal levels of respect.
However, the state may find it impossible to promote
equal respect among its citizens, since the psychological
processes which go into shaping people's attitudes and
beliefs may not be amenable to social engineering. How
then can we justify the use of the state as a
redistributive mechanism?

The principle that will license the conclusion is
one which appeals to the consent of the citizens to the
state's activity, where this consent is expressed through
the representative democratic process. Rawls (1972,
pp. 195-257) has shown that the institutions of representative government would be the type of political
system agreed under the social contract. To this extent

they represent just institutions of government.   If
consent is expressed through those institutions to the
redistributive activity of the state, then this will
license the judgment that the state ought to promote
the pursuit of a just distribution of welfare.

The legitimate extension of state activity therefore
depends upon prior consent by citizens.   It seems to me
(parenthetically) that this gives a coherent interpretation to the Rawlsian requirement that the equal liberty
principle be made lexicographically prior to the
principle governing the distribution of economic benefits.
Rawls (and his critics) are inclined to interpret this
requirement as the claim that large increments of
economic well-being should be sacrificed for quite
minute losses of civil liberties.   However, a more
realistic interpretation is the view that the legitimacy
of government action in the economic sphere depends
upon the prior consent they obtain through the ballot
box.   In this sense only are the constitutional liberties
lexicographically prior to the improvement of economic
welfare.

If democratic consent is at least a necessary condition for the state to promote an equal distribution of
welfare, then this is itself a pointer to the truth
contained in the entitlement theory of justice.   End-
state principles of justice, of whatever type, favour a
particular distribution of welfare, without, it seems,
considering the manner and means by which it is brought
about.   Ethically, however, it is surely relevant how
a particular distribution is brought about.   If a
thoroughly equal distribution of resources is created
by theft and pillage, this may be less satisfactory,
ethically, than a less equal distribution engineered by
constitutional means.   In stressing the ethical
importance of the *process* by which people come to
acquire their holdings, the entitlement theory has drawn
attention to an important aspect of distributive justice.
However, the entitlement theory of itself, provides no
reasons why people should not be concerned with the
distribution of welfare consequent upon free economic
exchange.   Equally it provides no argument against
people choosing to bring about a particular distribution
of welfare and implementing their decisions by means of
the political process. (3)

2   THE STATE AND SOCIAL POLICY

One argument against the state provision of social
services is that this can lead to the state becoming too
powerful. Fears have been expressed that the growth of
state power in this respect will lead to contraventions
of the rights of individuals (Rescher, 1972, p. 119).
Moreover, it has been suggested that a similar danger
arises whenever the attempt is made to introduce an
ordering into the distribution of benefits (Acton,
1971, pp. 63-5; Nozick, 1974, p. 163). On this
argument the egalitarian is inevitably driven toward
authoritarianism.

It is of course true that under conditions of free
exchange there is no one person who is responsible for
ordering the distribution of benefits. We are not in
the position of children who are each to be given a
portion of cake by some independent arbiter of our
entitlements. However, the proponent of distributive
justice does not hold that there is such an arbiter, who
has, so to speak, made the wrong decisions. Rather
the person who favours a patterned principle of distribution, like equality, believes that the conditions
under which market exchange takes place do not of
themselves provide an entitlement for the participants
of an exchange to an amount proportional to their
respective marginal products. In rewarding labour
outputs the market fails to provide for individual
entitlements to the social product stipulated by the
principles of justice. If the state is an effective
means of redistributing the benefits of exchange, then
there is no reason *in principle* why the egalitarian
objects to the use of state power for redistributive
ends, although he may believe that there are pragmatic
disadvantages in the growth of such power and the
development of bureaucracy.

There are, in fact, two possible types of danger
arising from the growth of state power, both of which
have been overemphasised by those who oppose redistributive measures. The first type of danger is that a
redistributive state will become powerful enough to
undermine constitutional and economic liberties. The
second is that the bureaucratic process of redistribution
will itself serve to deny people their rights, a
criticism that has been made by left, as well as right
wing critics of the welfare state.

On the first danger there is no evidence of any
causal connection between the growth of state power over
welfare and the undermining of constitutional and

economic freedoms. If anything, the evidence points in
the opposite direction. Sweden, for example, has been
a consistently high spender on welfare programmes, as
measured by the size of the social security budget (ILO,
1972, pp. 317-23), but as a country maintains a vigorous
private sector in the economy. In 1972, only 20 per cent
of the work-force was directly employed by the state and
the public sector controlled only 15 per cent of total
production of goods and services (Lansbury, 1972, p. 14).
Britain, by contrast a country with much lower levels
of welfare expenditure, employs about 30 per cent of the
total workforce in the public sector. These are admittedly
crude comparisons in some respects, since they ignore
some important features of Swedish economic management
which give it control over industry. But they hardly
support the case that high welfare spending and economic
authoritarianism go hand in hand. Moreover, there is
little evidence that equality and political authoritarianism go hand in hand. The maintenance of constitutional liberties depends on the political culture
rather than the redistributive activities of the state.
The Netherlands, another country high on welfare spending,
could hardly be described as politically authoritarian. (4)

Perhaps, it may be admitted, there is no direct
relationship between authoritarianism and equality.
However, it is still possible to argue that the
bureaucratic process of redistribution has its own
dangers. Both the man-in-the-house rule in American
social security programmes and the cohabitation rule
of the British Supplementary Benefit system for example
have been applied to the detriment of the individual's
right to privacy. But in this sort of case it is a matter
of ensuring that there is an independent, effective and
impartial administrative review which is capable of
reversing administrative decisions. Moreover, arbitrary
exercises of power can occur in the private sector. For
example it often takes strong trade union or professional
association pressure to insure that widows' benefits
are adequate under private superannuation schemes. In
this respect there is no reason for a general presumption
that state-provided services are inferior.

One specific objection which has been raised in
this context is that redistributive activity necessarily
involves *continuous* bureaucratic activity on the part
of the state. To decide to intervene in the market
outcome of benefits leaves the problem of when such
intervention is justified. Should people be allowed
to keep the benefits of exchange for a month, a week,
a day or how long? Logically, the egalitarian seems

driven to the conclusion that any gap in redistribution should be avoided. Thus Nozick (1974, p. 163) argues, 'no end-state principle or distributional patterned principle of justice can be *continuously* realized without *continuous* interference in people's lives.' (My emphasis.)

However, this statement is only true, if the egalitarian conceives the state as regulating the conditions of each economic transaction. But, as I have already argued (chapter 6.1), the principle of equality is taken to govern the fundamental economic institutions of a society, not the finest details of individual transactions. By the state confining its activities to the regulation of the general system of economic transactions, no problem of continuous interference need arise. One does not have to be over sanguine about the operations of the PAYE system to doubt that it represents an illegitimate extension of the Inland Revenue's power, resulting in detailed, continuous interference in people's lives.

There is, moreover, no reason why publicly-funded social services should automatically lead to an increase in the *state's* power. Educational vouchers are a clear example of state funding being combined with independent management and control of the educational system. In addition, *local* government currently administers a number of the social services, and though the local authorities are dependent upon central government for the bulk of their revenue, this is due largely to the antiquated sources of local government finance. The benefits of public and collective provision of the social services may equally be obtained under local or regional control as under central state control. The devolution of more powers down to the local level should assuage the fears of those who hold that the state's power is growing too great because it controls too large an area of social life.

One objection to greater local devolution of this type is that based on the conception of territorial justice (Davies, 1968, pp. 15-16). The argument here is that greater local autonomy in the social services results in unacceptable variations in the standards of social service provision between different regions. But there are two questions to be raised here. Are there no methods for coping with regional variations within the framework of local autonomy? And, are all local variations in standards of service undesirable in any case? Certainly, there may be cases where one feels it to be important that similar standards of service

are provided, domiciliary facilities for the physically
handicapped are a clear example: there seems to be no
reason why a handicapped person in one area of the
country should enjoy a lower standard of service than a
similarly placed person in another area of the country,
simply because the local authority chooses to implement
a different policy. But it will be possible for the
central government to specify standards of service which
local authorities should meet, without taking direct
control over those services.

The advantage of some degree of local autonomy is
that it does enable experimentation on different methods
of providing the same service. The important point here
is that local authorities may be in a better position
than central government for using different 'mixes' of
service to achieve the same output. For example,
social service departments provide domiciliary care for
the elderly and the handicapped. But a local authority
may well find it more efficient to spend more on housing
in order to provide similar care in domestic units which
are substitutable between different uses. The logic
of such co-ordination, as Klein (1975, p. 7) points out,
is *more* local discretion, i.e., the diffusion, rather
than the concentration, of government power. (The
trouble for the proponents of greater local autonomy
comes when we look at the structure of local government.
With the exception of the seven metropolitan areas, the
social service and housing departments are split between
two tiers of the English system. Does this provide a
reason for further central government intervention to
reform, once again, local government?)

Moreover, not all variations in local services need
violate the principles of social justice, at least as
defined by the egalitarian. If we simply think of
social justice as distribution according to need, then
variations in local services will be unjust, because
there will be two people with similar needs in different
localities who may not be receiving the same service.
But, as I have argued previously (chapter 5.2),
distribution according to need is not sufficient as a
definition of justice. What matters is that needs are
satisfied up to an equal level of benefit, where the
appropriate level of satisfaction is defined by the
consent of those affected through the political process.
The advantage of local autonomy here is that people may
express consent to different types of service in
different regions.

Wilensky (1975, pp. 52-3) has argued that there is
a strong correlation between high social policy

expenditure and the degree of authority the central
government has over local and regional units. There is
also a connection between programme emphasis on equality
and the degree of central control. The greater the
level of central control, the higher is public
expenditure on social policy benefits and the more equal
is the distribution of benefits. Thus, of the top nine
welfare-spending leaders, six are among the nine most
centralised governments (Belgium, the Netherlands, France,
Italy, East Germany and Czechoslovakia) and one is
ambiguous (Sweden, with a medium score on centralisation).
It seems that the proponent of social policy should
logically favour the strengthening of central state power.

However, this conclusion would be too strong for the
premise on which it is based. (Wilensky himself does
not draw any prescriptive conclusions.) At best the
evidence shows that there is some correlation between
centralisation and high welfare spending, but of itself
it does not explain why there should be such a correlation
or even whether the correlation is spurious or not.
The existence of striking exceptions to the generalisation
(both West Germany and Austria spend too much for their
low scores on centralisation) indicate that there is
no simple link between the characteristics of the
political system and the amount spent on social policy.
Centralisation seems neither a necessary condition
(Germany and Austria) nor a sufficient condition (Britain)
of high public spending on the social services. Other
factors seem just as important, including the ethnic
and religious diversity of the society in question.
The most one can conclude from Wilensky's figures is
that there may be unforeseen dangers for the egalitarian
in extending the range of local autonomy. Whether such
dangers would be significant in Britain, with its social
homogeneity and unified political culture, is a matter
for further empirical investigation, and does not raise
important issues of principle.

Local autonomy does not therefore necessarily result
in variations in service provision which are contrary to
the principles of social justice. This is not in itself
an argument for extending local autonomy, but such an
extension might well be considered by those who are
fearful of the growing power of the state as a result
of its intervention to promote greater equality. My
own opinion (for what it is worth) is that the dangers of
state control *and* local autonomy are overstressed from
both points of view, and whether one favours greater
local control of the social services will depend on
quite different sorts of factors: how willing people

will be to participate in political control at the local
level; how tight the supply is for skilled administrators; and how easy it is to provide a reasonably buoyant
source of revenue for local government. These sorts of
questions, however, have no essential bearing on the
role of equality in the social services.

3   SOCIAL POLICY AND THE MARKET

In discussing the general institutional structure of
a just society, I assumed that a competitive market
system could operate satisfactorily alongside a comprehensive system of state transfers and provision in
kind. The market system will allocate benefits according
to the criterion of economic efficiency; and the
transfer system will distribute benefits according to
considerations of welfare. However, it has been objected
(Acton, 1971, pp. 48-9) that there is an inconsistency
in using the social welfare system to promote equality
whilst allowing the market to operate on unequal
returns, even when these are subject to progressive
income tax. In particular, it is objected that the
provision of certain free services undermines the
structure of incentives on which the competitive
market economy rests. For what matters with incentives
presumably is not simply that some people are allowed
to earn nominally more than others, but that their
increase in earnings results in an improvement to their
standard of living. Moreover, if part of the rationale
for the egalitarian's concentration upon the social
services is that these are primary goods, whose consumption ought to be protected for all individuals, then
the argument against the dual system of market inequality
and welfare equality seems to become stronger: for
people are, *ex hypothesi*, deprived of the incentive to
work to provide for themselves in the most important
areas of private consumption.
  With respect to the issue of compatibility between
an incentive-oriented economy and a social welfare
system there are really two sets of important considerations, namely the undermining of incentives caused by
high marginal rates of taxation on earned income to
finance social welfare benefits and second the extent
to which the provision of such benefits weakens
people's incentive to work and provide for themselves.
On the first type of consideration it is important
to note that there is no theoretical reason why high
marginal tax rates should lead to a reduction of work

effort. The effect of high tax rates for each individual
is to raise the price of income relative to leisure.
Whether this leads to a reduction of work effort,
however, depends on the preference schedules of the
individual involved. At the new price ratio for
income and leisure an individual may *increase* his work
effort (cf. Brown, 1968). For example, if he wishes
to preserve a certain standard of living net of tax,
then an increase in the price of income relative to
leisure will lead to a decrease in the amount of
leisure consumed, and a corresponding increase in work
effort. It is impossible to predict in practice what
the result will be of high marginal tax rates unless
one has evidence on people's preference schedules.
Moreover, even if the empirical evidence suggested that
individuals were deterred from work effort one would
still need to know by how much different tax rates
affected their work activity before one judged that
the disadvantages of high taxation rates outweighed the
advantages of the social welfare system.

With respect to the weakening of incentives to work,
here again there are a number of plausible conjectures
which require more evidence before we can decide between
them. It may be that people will work harder if they
know that a lot depends upon their own personal
initiative. On the other hand people may be less
willing to take risks unless they are guaranteed a
'safety net' of services which will protect them should
they fail. Moreover, some social policy provision may
be important in encouraging mobility of labour, by
removing a disincentive upon people moving from one
area to another. Equalising the quality of housing, for
instance, may remove one barrier in the way of people
moving from one region to another. Once again, the
exact effect of the social services is impossible to
predict in the absence of any detailed knowledge of
individual utility functions and preference schedules.

There are, then, no reasons for thinking that a
social welfare transfer system is necessarily inconsistent
with the workings of a market economy. However, an
elaborate social welfare system may create political
and economic instability indirectly through its effects
on the government's management of the economy. To see
why this is so it is necessary to look at the degree
of popular support a government will receive for
increasing welfare spending.

It has sometimes been argued that a social system
based on end-state principles of justice will be stable
because people will see that the pooling of natural

advantages includes everyone's good in a scheme of
mutual benefit. Support for the system will therefore
stem from self-interest, since persons will be aware
that the community will support them in time of need
in exchange for an agreement by individuals to contribute
their share to the pool of social benefits. The trouble
with this argument is that the main beneficiaries of
social policy programmes tend to be minority groups
within the population - the old, handicapped and single
parent families for example. There is no incentive for
a majority of the population to subscribe to egalitarian
social policy programmes, since in the absence of a
public commitment to equality they would be better
off. And, although there is correspondingly an incentive
on the part of the worst-off members of the population
to affirm their allegiance to a social system which
includes their good in a scheme of mutual well-being,
they are not numerically significant enough to ensure
the stability of the dual system of allocation and
distribution which supports them.

To some extent majority dissatisfaction with an
egalitarian system is off-set by certain specific
factors. There is, for example, the 'money illusion',
by which people are more aware of the nominal value of
their gross incomes than they are of their real disposable income (Dobb, 1969, p. 63). Moreover, if welfare
benefits are financed out of indirect, rather than direct,
taxation, there is less resistance to increases in
spending, just as there is similarly less resistance if
the social distance between middle- and low-income groups
is small (Wilensky, 1975, pp. 52-69). However, even
the effect of these off-setting factors is liable to
diminish the more the social welfare system moves
towards a greater degree of equality.

The suggestion was made earlier (p. 107) that an
end-state distribution required legitimation through
the political process if it was to be just not simply
in its results but also in the manner by which it is
established. So long as this requirement is maintained
in practice, as well as being held ethically desirable,
it might be thought that the stability of the dual
system would be maintained: the majority would consent
to any extension of welfare spending, and this would
presumably be an expression of internalised norms of
social justice. However, in a competitive two-party
system not even the requirement of democratic consent
is sufficient to stabilise a distributive transfer
system on top of a competitive market economy.
Specific institutional restraints are necessary if

the system is to be viable.

To see why this is so one must look at the position of individual parties within a competitive framework. It has been frequently remarked that political parties who are anxious to increase welfare spending face a dilemma. In order to finance welfare benefits they have to impose tax burdens upon the majority of the population including many of their own supporters. (5) Indeed even political parties who are not ideologically committed to an increase in welfare spending may find themselves in a similar dilemma if they simply want to maintain the quality of the existing welfare system. The explanation of this dilemma is found in the 'relative price effect' by which the costs of the social services, with their high labour input, tend to rise faster than general costs in the economy. A political party in office, therefore, finds itself in a zero-sum situation, facing a trade-off between its commitment to welfare spending and its desire to retain the support of the electorate.

In such a situation a political party, concerned to secure a required share of the popular vote, will aim to transform the zero-sum trade-off into a more manageable problem. One method of doing this is to increase the rate of economic growth, financing welfare spending out of the increments to national income. However, growth cannot always be guaranteed, and governments cannot always directly secure the structural changes in the economy which would move it onto increasing levels of productivity. The alternative, in a non-growth or sluggish growth situation, is to finance increases in welfare spending by a budgetary deficit, leaving personal consumption at existing levels. The same result might also arise if the government expands the money supply in an attempt to maintain full employment. If wage and salary earners aim to increase real disposable incomes by covering tax and social security payments through increased money incomes, the natural result in the absence of any government intervention, is to increase unemployment. However, a government fearful of unemployment will increase spending capacity in order to off-set the increased cost of workers, and this will result in inflation.

Whatever the mechanism behind the growth of the budget deficit - be it a direct link between social welfare expansion and spending or an indirect link between inflationary wage pressures to off-set taxation and public spending - the result in the long-term is not simply an increase in prices, but inflation at an increasing rate (Brittan, 1969, p. 464) and, if this is a consequence of the dual system of market inequality and social welfare equality, there seems to be good reason for saying that the system is unstable, or at least that the political system on which it is based will be significantly weakened by consequent inflationary pressures.

The central problem is coping with the conflicting demands, within a competitive political system, between personal consumption and the social welfare system, without creating an inflationary budgetary deficit. In order to achieve this aim, it would be valuable were the public authorities to commit themselves to a rule for the expansion in money supply, stated either in terms of the total stock of money (Friedman, 1962, p. 55) or in terms of the total level of demand for home-produced goods and services (Meade, 1975, p. 34), whichever was judged the most appropriate. Decisions on the distribution of resources between public and private consumption could then be made within this general framework for expansion. Moreover, in order further to separate the political decisions involved, it would also be valuable to institute a Stabilisation Commission of the sort advocated by Meade (ibid., p. 40), which would be responsible for making medium-term adjustments of the money supply, as the Central Bank is now responsible for making day-to-day adjustments. Naturally such a Commission would have to operate within the general framework of monetary expansion proposed by the governing political party, and to that extent there is no ultimately independent source of monetary control apart from the competitive political process. But an independent Commission might well develop enough political authority to prevent the expansion of the money supply being used as an unwise tool of policy. And, in any case, the fact that under such an arrangement the governing party would have to make a public commitment to a specified rate of expansion in domestic monetary facilities itself would act as a source of criticism and opposition should it then renege on its previous commitment.

The effect of these reforms would be to weaken those pressures on the party system which lead to its becoming unstable by virtue of its commitment to high social welfare spending. Because the governing political party would still have to be left with final control over social and economic policy, there is no way by which the inflationary pressures are firmly controlled, in the absence of political parties either securing or fortuitously experiencing in their term of office a

high rate of economic growth. There are reasons therefore
for thinking that Acton may be right in supposing that
the mixture between market inequality and welfare equality
is unstable, *provided the argument is stated with
reference to the current competitive party system*.
However, with suitable reforms, it should be possible
to avoid the worst pit-falls of party competition.
Given the appropriate set of institutional arrangements,
there is no reason why an adequate transfer branch of
government should operate unsuccessfully within the
economic limits determined by the political parties,
and there is no reason for thinking that the transfer
branch could not effectively pursue the goal of
equality.

4   ALTRUISM, CITIZENSHIP AND SOCIAL POLICY

Having described the sort of institutional framework
within which an egalitarian social policy might be
pursued, I have in the last two sections been discussing
objections to such a set of institutions with their
attendant disadvantages. In this section I should
like to conclude this institutional discussion by
examining two arguments which have been advanced *in
favour* of the sort of institutions which I have assumed.
The purpose of this discussion is to suggest that neither
argument is valid and that the strongest arguments
therefore in favour of the type of social welfare
programmes I have been discussing remain the pure
distributive considerations in terms of social justice.
    One argument which is sometimes used to defend a
structure of state social services against competitive
market provision is that their being free at the point
of delivery to those in need encourages greater
efficiency because it encourages additional voluntary
altruistic help towards the cost of the social services.
This argument can be expressed as follows. Under a
market system the amount of resources devoted to the
social services will be dependent on the effective demand
for those services. Under a state financed system the
amount of resources will be determined by the proportion
of the social product devoted to those services.
However, there is a greater altruistic element in the
state system, and this will be apparent to people. This
in itself will encourage voluntary help in the social
services, because it will give people an opportunity
to express their own altruism. This extra voluntary
work, being unpaid, will increase the outputs for the

same number of inputs, and therefore will register as an
efficiency increase. Thus it can be argued that payment
for blood donations would itself be a deterrent to
people giving blood voluntarily, and may be less
efficient for that reason (Titmuss, 1970, p. 224).

However, all that this argument establishes is that
the state services may be more efficient for this reason
than comparable services in the market, not that they
must be so. The proper comparison is between the total
social service outputs that are created by the private
market, and the total outputs that issue from the state
system. The second may be greater than the first for
the same inputs, but there is no guarantee that this will
be so, and whether or not it is will depend on a great
many empirical factors. Moreover, the argument also
makes the tacit assumption that market provision will
put an end to altruistic voluntary help in the social
services. But why should this be so? At best therefore
the argument will only establish that the social services
may be more efficient under state provision for this
reason, and whether or not this is true will depend on
empirical circumstances.

It might also be argued that, although a state-cum-
voluntary system was no more efficient than a market
system, the social relationships which it encouraged
were intrinsically more desirable than those fostered
within a market system. This is possibly true, although
it is difficult to see what available empirical evidence
would support the argument. Moreover, state administered
services have significant disadvantages, most notably
that many cases of welfare entitlement must be left to
officials to decide within the limits of their own
discretion. There is no reason to think that the quality
of the relationship prevailing between official and
recipient is likely to be any higher than that obtaining
between seller and buyer in a market system.

One positive benefit which has been claimed for the
state provision of the social services is that it
promotes a sense of equal citizenship. Just as the
granting of certain political rights (the right to vote,
participate in elections and form political alliances)
was essential in creating the equal status of all persons
as political citizens, so the granting of certain social
rights (the entitlement to social security, health
care and free education in particular) is essential to
complementing this citizenship and securing equality of
social status for all members of the society (cf. Marshall,
1950, p. 56).

Within the contractarian argument which I have been

developing rights of any kind are themselves to be
counted as benefits distributed under the principles of
justice. The advantage of looking at social rights in
this way is that the principles of justice provide a
means of circumscribing or delimiting the rights which
people hold. The question of what social rights people
have can be answered by reference to the principles of
distribution and the theory of primary goods. People
have such social rights as would guarantee them a share
of primary goods determined by the principles of
distributive justice.

   In understanding the relationship between social
rights and social status, this grounding of social rights
in the theory of justice becomes particularly important.
To appreciate this it is necessary first to note that
there is an analytic connection between citizens having
equal rights of political participation and their sharing
equality of citizenship. Equal citizenship in the
dimension of political power means that all people in
society enjoy the same rights. By contrast, the
granting of similar social rights to all citizens does
not of itself guarantee equality of status. What matters
is not simply that all citizens are given a right to X,
but that they are given a right to a specific amount of
X. Equality of status cannot be secured until people
believe that the shares they have been allocated are
the shares to which they are in justice entitled. In
other words there is not an analytic connection between
having equal social rights and sharing equal citizenship.
What matters is not simply that people have rights, but
that they have rights to specified levels of benefit.
The sense of equal citizenship is only promoted when
people believe that the social rights they are given
correspond to portions they would be allocated under the
principles of justice. In order for social rights to
promote a sense of equal citizenship it is first necessary
that people believe the allocation of rights is just.

   However, it does not follow from this argument
that people will think that equal levels of welfare are
their just entitlement. People may hold views on
justice in which, for example, they are only entitled to
a minimum subsistence share of the social product.
Alternatively, people may feel their social status is
enhanced only when they are not dependent upon others
for support. Out of a sense of self-respect the poor
may not wish to feel dependent upon state officials for
an improvement in their material well-being. If the
least well-off members of society hold to such views,
then they have no reason to feel that any distribution

of social rights which grants them less ~~~~
denies them equal citizenship. They are
equally as citizens, since each person ⫶
due under a certain conception of justic⫶

The argument from equal citizenship ca⫶
by itself, therefore, as an argument for th⫶
greater economic equality in the social servi⫶
order to achieve that conclusion it is necessary ⫶
some further premises concerning the beliefs and
attitudes which people have about their legitimate
entitlements. More importantly, however, without any
information on citizens' beliefs and attitudes, the
argument of equal citizenship cannot be used to establish
that the institutions of the welfare state promote a
sense of equal citizenship. People may hold desert-
based notions of justice, in which their entitlements
are given as a reward for their own actions and efforts.
If this is their attitude, then the institutions of the
welfare state may not promote equal status. Instead
they may be regarded as counter-productive to the
promotion of justice.

None of this argument implies that the promotion of
equality of status is not a justified goal of the welfare
services. It only shows that the justice of an equal
distribution of prestige must be established by independent argument. Given that it can be so established,
then there will be an obligation upon the public
services to act in accordance with it, for example by
acting with civility towards the recipients of welfare
benefits. Moreover, although the promotion of economic
equality does not follow strictly from the promotion
of equal social status, it will be an argument for
greater economic equality, if it is true that members
of the population link the two together. If those who
are habitually poor are regarded as socially inferior
by members of society because of their poverty, then
the promotion of more equal prestige will involve the
promotion of greater economic equality.

I conclude, then, that the possession of certain
universal social rights, e.g., the right to Supplementary
Benefit within the British welfare system, does not
necessarily grant its holders equality of social status.
Much depends upon the exact nature of the right, what
the entitlement allows, the type of institution that is
used to meet the right, how much discretion public
officials are allowed and so on. Just as there is no
direct implication from the claim that people should
share equality of status to the claim that they should
share equal levels of economic welfare, so there is no

ation from the claims of equal status to a
mendation for any particular type of social
fare institution.

The promotion of a sense of equal citizenship is an
important goal for public policy, and public institutions
should be designed in order to achieve that end. Hence,
a just society might be characterised as one in which
there was a confluence among all those social practices
implied by the principles of justice. Practices which
promoted equality in the dimensions of power, status and
life-chances would then be mutually reinforcing. However,
in the design of actual social welfare systems, it may
prove impossible to attain this optimum arrangement.
The alternative is to appeal to the argument that, as
primary goods, social policy benefits should be
distributed so as to promote an equal distribution
of welfare.

Notes

CHAPTER 1 INTRODUCTION

1 This last goal has been increasingly questioned in
   recent years. For a good critique see Mishan (1969).
   There is, of course, a problem as to what constitutes
   growth. Mishan's work can be read as a criticism
   of those who equate a growth in physical output with
   a growth in welfare. However, it is probably true
   to say that this equation has been assumed in most
   political discussions of economic policy.
2 Full employment will be a means if it is regarded as
   one way of promoting growth by encouraging investment
   through a high level of effective demand.
3 Cf. the following remarks by Geoffrey Howe:
        It is one thing to say that something is
        unfair, that we want to try and do something about
        it, or that this degree of poverty, this degree of
        exclusion of access to society is plainly
        intolerable and something has to be done about
        that. If you turn that sense of seeking for a
        more contented, more coherent, more just society,
        into the pursuit of equality, then you start down
        the road to many fallacies, particularly when you
        pursue economic equality (quoted from a
        conversation in Vaizey, 1975, pp. 50-1).
4 In order to avoid repetition I shall sometimes use
   the terms 'social welfare policy' or 'the social
   services' instead of social policy. The former is
   unfortunate because it suggests it has a connotation
   with the economists' social welfare function, and
   the latter is unfortunate because it may be confused
   with the personal social services. Whenever there
   is a possibility of misunderstanding I shall refer
   to social policy.

5 Calculated from 'Public Expenditure to 1979-80' (1976)
   Table 1.4, p. 14.
6 Butler and Stokes (1974, pp. 296-302) do show a
   decline in the salience of social welfare issues
   among the electorate between 1963 and 1970, but even
   in 1970 the impact of these issues is high. For
   some people social welfare is salient because they
   believe that less money should be spent on it.
   For example 2 per cent of respondents wanted family
   allowances to go only to the needy. Nevertheless,
   in 1970 about 30 per cent of the electorate thought
   social welfare issues the most important facing
   the government in terms which suggested they
   favoured increased spending. See Butler and
   Stokes (1974, Table 14.1, p. 297).
7 For an early attempt to assess the total impact of
   government spending see Barna (1945). For a modern
   study cf. Nicholson (1974).
8 For example, one line of argument stresses the
   transideological significance of the welfare
   state, and sees social policy as a way of reducing
   inequalities. Bell (1960, p. 373) writes:
       In the Western world, therefore, there is today
       a rough consensus among intellectuals on political
       issues: the acceptance of the Welfare State; the
       desirability of decentralised power; a system of
       mixed economy and political pluralism.
   For a similar appraisal of the welfare state compare
   e.g. Strachey (1952). But there is really very
   little consensus on how far the welfare state, and
   social policy in particular, should be used to
   promote *equality*. Thus even Crosland, a thinker
   sympathetic to the ideal, said in 'The Future of
   Socialism' (1956, p. 113):
       The relief of distress and the elimination of
       ... squalor is the main object of social
       expenditure; and a socialist is identified as
       one who wishes to give this an exceptional
       priority over other claims on resources. This
       is not a matter of the overall vertical equality
       of incomes; the arguments are humanitarian and
       compassionate, not egalitarian.
   This contrasts with the views of Saville (1957) and
   Titmuss (1965). For a summary of competing political
   evaluations of the welfare state, with special
   reference to social policy, see Wedderburn (1965) and
   for other interesting discussions see the publications
   by the Institute for Economic Affairs. For political
   disagreement on social policy in the USA see Rein
   (1970, pp. 21-43).

CHAPTER 2   PROCEDURAL EQUALITY

1   This double-barrelled principle is an amalgam of the
    formulations of the principle frequently canvassed
    in the literature. For the first part of the
    principle cf. Bedau (1967, p. 19); Benn and Peters
    (1959, p. 110) and Stephen (1896, p. 185); and for
    the second part see Beardsley (1964, p. 35); Bowie
    (1970, pp. 140-1); Blackstone (1967, p. 240);
    Lucas (1965, pp. 296-7). Berlin (1956, pp. 302-3)
    and Flathman (1967) cite both parts of the principle,
    as does von Leyden (1963).
2   I am grateful to Dorothy Emmet for suggesting this
    connection between the idea of procedural equality
    and the notion of defeasibility. She is not, of
    course, responsible for the analysis that I offer of
    the connection.
3   Hart's article has been criticised by some writers,
    most notably Geach (1960) and Pitcher (1960), and
    Hart himself has admitted in the preface to
    'Punishment and Responsibility' (1968) the force of
    these criticisms. I suspect he may have been too
    charitable in giving way so easily. Much of the
    criticism focuses upon the applicability of the
    notion of defeasibility to human action. Geach
    (op. cit., p. 224) for example, wants statements
    explaining actions to be causal. But Hart's thesis
    need not be taken to deny that explanations of
    human actions by reference to mental events are
    causal. Once we attend to his point that identifying
    ascription and *description* is confusing the belief
    that A was responsible for X, and the grounds on
    which we hold that belief (see above, p. 14), then
    we can fit in causal descriptive statements as the
    grounds for our ascription. In any case, even were
    the criticism valid, nothing follows about the notion
    of defeasibility, only about the correct domain of
    its application. The crucial question in the present
    context is whether it works to elucidate the concept
    of procedural equality.
4   Though it should be noted that Dorothy Emmet uses
    this notion in a rather different context to one in
    which I am using it here, applying it to Rawls'
    original position.
5   For example, Hart (1961, p. 156) offers part (b) of
    the notion of procedural equality, which as I have
    already remarked is close in some ways to the 'good
    reason' condition, as one of the 'principles of
    Natural Justice'. As such it provides one means

for guaranteeing impartiality - non-arbitrariness as
we might say.

6 There are a number of other contexts in which
treatment is the good being distributed. This seems
to be particularly true, for example, in the case
of racial discrimination. Here again the emphasis
seems to be on non-arbitrariness in the way
people are treated.

7 Cf. Sidgwick (1874, p. 267):

it is plain that laws may be equally executed
and yet unjust: for example, we should consider
a law unjust which compelled only red-headed
men to serve in the army, even though it were
applied with the strictest impartiality to all
red-haired men.

Note that in this example part (a) of the condition
of procedural equality is ignored.

8 Cf. 'Proposals for a Tax-Credit System' (1972), and
Hansard, 'Parliamentary Debates', 13 May, 1975, cols
330-406.

9 See Keynes (1940, pp. 399-400). For this reference
to Keynes' views on the subject of child tax
allowances I am grateful to Lynes (1971, pp. 118-19).
It is not strictly correct nowadays to refer to
'surtax payers', as I do in the subsequent discussion,
as surtax has been abolished. But it remains a
convenient way of referring to those persons who
pay the highest rate of tax.

10 For a discussion of the relationship between taxation
and housing policy, see Netzer (1967).

11 From approximately 90 per cent to 15 per cent of
the market.

12 This is probably not true in the case of increased
rebates or allowances to tenants who are renting,
however. I am grateful to Ken Judge for discussion
on this point.

CHAPTER 3   SUBSTANTIVE EQUALITY

1 I shall assume that the problem is to allocate the
benefits of social co-operation rather than the
burdens and benefits. This is a simplifying
assumption, made on the basis that the burdens of
social co-operation will be outweighed by the
benefits, so that it is legitimate to talk just
about the distribution of benefits, when what is
meant is net benefit.

2 For the principle of equal constitutional liberties

see Rawls (1972, pp. 195-257); on social status
see Runciman (1967).

3 By the term 'welfare' I understand the total set of
satisfactions a person derives from living in any
given social state. The notion can be operationally
defined if we say that a person's welfare will be
higher in social state A than in social state B, if
he would prefer to live in A rather than B given
perfect knowledge concerning his tastes, future
personality and the outcomes of alternative social
states, and given also no systematic time preference
by which future satisfactions are discounted at a
higher rate than present satisfactions of the same
value.

4 Cf; Godwin (1798, p. 86): 'We have in reality
nothing that is strictly speaking our own. We have
nothing that has not a destination prescribed to it
by the immutable voice of reason and justice.'

CHAPTER 4   PRIMARY GOODS AND SOCIAL POLICY

1 For a discussion of some of the institutional problems
which arise over the distinction between $incentives_1$
and $incentives_2$ see chapter 7.1.

2 Cf. Sen (1973, p. 17). For a discussion of the
concept of need, cf. chapter 5.

3 Cf. the survey evidence which I cited in chapter 1
from Butler and Stokes (1974, pp. 296-302).

4 Cf. Nath (1968, p. 143):

What if only a certain sub-group has a taste for
a special kind of wine in the making of which so
much time and skill are spent that it will be
produced only if a high price could be paid for
it and which that sub-group cannot afford to pay?
The answer depends on the adopted social welfare
function of the community for taking decisions.
The same community might decide against any
special assistance for this group, as decides
in favour of free hearing aids for the deaf
or free musical concerts. And yet there is no
reason why according to the *individual* social
welfare function (of some person or persons)
these might not be wrong decisions.

That Nath includes musical concerts in benefits
to be redistributed underlines the point that a
list of such benefits depends upon value judgments,
although of course a social welfare function may be
based on various considerations not all of which

need be framed in terms of principles of distributive justice.

5   Note that there is nothing irrational about a person buying some services from the government in exchange for taxation. Nor does he necessarily have to be submitting himself to a paternal authority. The citizen 'buying' state services may just be reducing his information costs and the uncertainty involved in shopping on the open market. For example, it could pay a person to enter a state superannuation scheme, even though it provided fewer benefits than a private scheme, if the state scheme were fully inflation-proofed and the private scheme was not.

6   'Primary' poverty is that caused by an absolute lack of financial resources relative to need or conventional standards of living. 'Secondary' poverty arises through the mismanagement of otherwise adequate resources.

7   Though I would not want to claim it as lexico-graphically prior to the second rule of justice, be it a difference principle or equality or whatever, as does Rawls.

8   Two successive Secretaries of State for Social Services have wanted to even out the provision of resources. Sir Keith Joseph said he wanted to *eradicate* inequalities in the services available in different areas. ('Public Expenditure to 1977-78', 1973, Cmnd 5519, p. 98) and Mrs Barbara Castle said 'further efforts will be made to *reduce* the inequalities in standards of service which exist between different areas' ('Public Expenditure to 1978-79', 1975, Cmnd 5879, p. 104) (italics added to both). It is interesting to find a Conservative Minister apparently being more radical than his Labour counter-part. (I owe these quotations to Judge, 1976, p. 127.)

9   Cf. Anderson (1972, p. 158):
    the dominant reason why the Swedish mortality rates are lower than in any state in the United States is a high minimum standard of living for everyone and a cultural homogeneity of life styles of sanitation and cleanliness. Health services are, of course, also a factor in the low mortality rates, but the elimination of poverty in the United States in the sense true for Sweden would be more likely to bring mortality rates closer to Sweden than a policy limited to health services only.... When the Swedes have as many private automotive vehicles

relatively as Americans, deaths from sedentary
causes may well rise.

10   To some extent the tendency to reward efficiency is
counter-balanced by the fact that the RHA formula
is based on a composite of indicators, with population
and case-flow weighted in the proportions three to one.

11   Cf. the ideological huffing and puffing in the final
words of the 1971 white paper (DHSS, 1971, p. 27):
'It is by personal enterprise and foresight, and not
by reliance on an ever-widening extension of State
commitments, that better living standards for our
people in the later years of life will be secured.'

12   Samuelson's argument is complex, but relies basically
on showing that there are two solutions for the
appropriate market-clearing equations representing
the transfer of resources between generations.
Under the first solution, interest rates will vary
with the growth rate of the population, but will
be finitely positive to allow transfers. Under the
second solution interest-rates are prohibitive
(negatively infinite) and so transfers will not
take place. The crux of the argument is to show
the second as the free market solution. The
reasoning here is intuitively straightforward.
A makes an agreement with B under which B pays A
during A's old age. B must get something in return,
namely someone to finance his consumption in old
age who may be called C. However, A can do nothing
for B in return either directly or indirectly through
an agreement with C, since when it comes to the time
for B and C to benefit in their retirement A will be
dead. A can only provide benefits in his productive
years, and these must go to someone older than
all three.

13   Sidgwick (1874, p. 273):
For, from one point of view, we are disposed to
think that the *customary* distribution, of rights,
goods and privileges, as well as burdens and
pains, is natural and just, and that this ought
to be maintained by law, as it usually is:
while from another point of view, we seem to
recognize an ideal system of rules of distribution
which ought to exist, but perhaps have never yet
existed, and we consider laws to be just in
proportion as they conform to this ideal.

14   See 'Proposals for a Tax-Credits Scheme' (1972).

CHAPTER 5   NEED AND EQUALITY

1   For the notion of extensional equivalence and its
    application to moral and political principles, see
    Lyons (1965).
2   It is therefore wrong to assert that social justice
    is distribution according to need, since the benefit
    to be distributed, i.e., the satisfaction of needs,
    is being confused with the rule under which the
    benefit is distributed.
3   Cf. the following by David Owen (1975, p. 6), when
    he was Minister of Health:
        People working in the health service have known
        for years that choices have had to be made.
        There is no health service in the world which
        does not have to define priorities. We have
        to face up to the fact that the demand is all
        embracing and we will never be able to meet it
        all.
4   Shortly after I wrote this chapter the government
    announced its intention of charging the full NHS cost
    of motor accidents to motor insurance companies.
    Although the social costs of treating car accidents
    can be assigned more easily than costs arising from
    a number of other risky activities, the principle
    of assigning costs in this way can not only be given
    a rationale within the theory of justice, but also
    has practical applications, as the car accident
    case shows.
5   Cf. Rothenberg (1961, pp. 316-17):   'The basic
    consensus extends to social validation of decision
    processes whose choices concern the social state
    alternatives of welfare economics; the consensus
    extends to a choice of an "official" Social
    Welfare Function.'
6   Cf. the evidence cited earlier on the political
    popularity of social welfare policy.
7   Cf. Rescher (1972, p. 4):
        Since welfare relates to the availability of the
        basic requisites for human well-being, it points
        towards the idea of a certain minimum level in the
        standard of living: any failure to achieve this
        level is thereby to be viewed as creating a
        corresponding·deficiency in point of welfare.
        The problem of specifying the setting of such a
        level, particularly in the pivotally important
        economic sector of welfare, is oviously a major
        issue in the theory of welfare.
    Note Rescher's logical slip in moving from the claim

that welfare theory is concerned with the minimum
necessary conditions for welfare, to the claim that
it ought only to be concerned with the provision of
minimum levels of service with respect to those
conditions.

8   Cf. Nozick (1974) for the notion of a time-slice
theory.

9   I ignore the difficult question of what children's
entitlements might be under a proliferation of
voluntary systems. Are their entitlements to be
judged on the basis of their parents' consent, or
should they be given the benefit of the doubt and
be made beneficiaries of the scheme without having
any corresponding obligations?

CHAPTER 6   INSTITUTIONS (1)

1   Cf. Friedman (1962, p. 15) on the advantages, as he
sees them, of a decentralised over a centralised
economic system:
  What the market does is to reduce greatly the
  range of issues that must be decided through
  political means, and thereby minimize the
  extent to which government need participate
  directly in the game. *The characteristic feature
  of action through political channels is that it
  tends to require or enforce substantial conformity.*
  The great advantage of the market, on the other
  hand, is that it permits wide diversity.
  (My emphasis.)

2   This help might take a variety of forms, e.g.,
reduced interest loans to private hospitals in poorly
served regions, or special capital grants to help
with new investment.

3   The figures are as follows for the period 1974-5.
Prescriptions accounted for 8.6 per cent of total
current expenditure and 7.8 per cent of total
expenditure. Hospital expenditure, both capital and
current, accounted for 81.2 per cent of expenditure
(figures calculated from 'Public Expenditure to
1979-80' (1976) pp. 93 and 95).

4   Cf. Plowden (1967, p. 57):
  We ask for 'positive discrimination'.... Schools
  in deprived areas should be given priority in
  many respects. The first steps must be to raise
  schools with low standards to the national
  average: the second, quite deliberately to make
  them better. The justification is that the

homes and neighbourhoods from which many of their children come provide little support and stimulus for learning. The schools must supply a compensating environment. The attempts so far made within the educational system to do this have not been sufficiently generous or sustained, because the handicaps imposed by the environment have not been explicitly and sufficiently allowed for. They should be.

5   The analogy is not quite accurate, since schools do not have the same spill-over effects as shops. For example, I understand that one leading chain store, specialising in durables, always seeks to place itself close to a leading food retailer if possible, since the spill-over custom is so advantageous. However, for present purposes I think the argument in the text stands.

6   Cf. the remarks of Dahl (1961, p. 146) on the consequences of high-status citizens in New Haven sending their children to private schools:

> [It] reduces the concern among the better educated elements in New Haven for standards of excellence in the public schools, and it creates among about a fifth of the parents a double load of costs for education - local taxes and private tuition - that generate latent opposition to increasing the outlays on public schools.

7   These points assume no change to a negative income tax or social dividend scheme.

CHAPTER 7   INSTITUTIONS (2)

1   For the importance of the distinction between the allocation and distribution of resources see Meade (1964, pp. 11-26).

2   Cf. Bergson (1967, pp. 662-3) on the wage structure of a socialist economic system, as advocated by Oscar Lange:

> Wage differentials in fact could be expected to correspond to differences in marginal utility only in equilibrium and there only for workers on the margin of choice between occupations. So far as there is disequilibrium or workers are intramarginal, their earnings have the character of rents, which by Lange's own standard, would be inequitable. As Lange recognized, rents would be particularly great for persons with rare talents, though he hoped, surely rather

optimistically, that these rents could be extracted by taxation without adverse effects on efficiency.

3 In his argument for the minimal state Nozick (1974) nowhere considers the argument that the electorate may want an extension of the state's power in order to achieve certain ends.

4 Cf. Wilensky (1975, p. 115):
Since World War II, civil liberties have surely not been threatened as much in the Netherlands and Sweden, countries at the top of any measure of welfare spending and output, as they have suffered in the United States, Canada and Japan, three of our welfare-state laggards. Indeed, the great tolerance and libertarian traditions of the Dutch have retained their vitality since the sixteenth century. And neither the Dutch or Swedes appear to lack either discipline or independence of spirit.

5 Cf. Marquand (1969, p. 490): The gap between the poor and the rest of society
can only be closed by a deliberate redistribution of income, away from the comfortable and toward the poor. In a democracy this can only be done if the majority - or at least a significant part of the majority - agree. And the moral of the last five years of British history (1964-69) is that the majority are not going to agree unless the overall rate of growth is high enough for their own living standards to improve in absolute terms while the redistribution is carried out.

Guide to further reading

Books on the subject of political argument and social
policy tend to fall into two classes: those by philosophers and political theorists dealing with political
argument and those by social administrators on social
policy. Two exceptions are Acton (1971) and Rescher
(1972). Both are written from a standpoint opposed to
the present volume, being disposed to place little
emphasis upon distributive justice as a goal of social
policy and more emphasis upon freedom and a corresponding
market remedy for the problems of allocation and
distribution. Their major fault is that both are strong
on assertion and weak on supporting evidence or argument.
In Acton's work, however, the reader will find a crisp
statement of a viewpoint at odds with the one presented
here. For a deeper philosophical presentation of a
similar political position Nozick (1974) should be
consulted, though it is marred by a failure to deal with
the moral foundations of a libertarian theory.

The best single work on the subject of political
argument is by Barry (1965). The main thesis of the
book - that all political arguments can be divided into
two types: want-regarding and ideal-regarding - is
less interesting than the detailed discussion of
particular topics. Those parts of the book concerned
with segregation and the Supreme Court, equality in
relation to schools and medical care, and the rationale
for child allowances are masterpieces of exposition and
detail. Lucas (1966) is another book aspiring to
offer a general analysis of political argument, but it
fails by comparison, partly because it does not discuss
enough real examples to enable one to see what is
implied by Lucas's own political commitment.

The foundation of the contract theory of justice is,
of course, to be found in Rawls (1972). Because Rawls

has modified, in various crucial respects, the arguments
found in his earlier articles, there really is no
substitute for reading the book itself. Moreover, there
are changes of emphases during the course of the book ,
and this means that there is no alternative to reading
the book the whole way through. It is, however, a work
which amply repays close and careful reading, and no
one who takes the trouble to become acquainted with it
should come away disappointed. It is best read in
conjunction with works which develop a similar approach,
like Harsanyi (1955) and Runciman (1966; 1967). The
two standard critical texts are by Barry (1973) and
Daniels (1975). But for the most incisive criticisms
the reader is probably best advised to look at Sen's
(1970, chapter 9) discussion of contract theories and
related approaches to the topic of distributive justice.

For a less detailed, but nevertheless informative
and lucid, discussion of the idea of justice and the
associated topic of rights, Raphael (1970) is well worth
looking at. Miller (1976) also offers a lucid account
of the idea of justice, distinguishing three components
of the idea: rights, needs and deserts. In respect
of needs, Miller puts forward an interesting interpretation of the concept, which may be contrasted with
the one presented here.

There are numerous articles written by philosophers
and political theorists on the subject of equality.
However, many of them are simply repetitive, and the
prospective reader is best advised to stick with three
classic articles by Mortimore (1968), Vlastos (1962)
and Williams (1962). The last, in particular, gives
an attractive presentation of the idea that it is a
claim to common humanity which underlies arguments for
equality. Sen (1973) discusses economic equality
specifically. Although the central chapters are taken
up with a detailed discussion of the statistical problems
surrounding measures of inequality, the first and last
chapters raise more general problems of political
argument concerning egalitarian ideals. The book is
particularly useful for its contrast between egalitarian
and utilitarian principles, which are frequently
confused in this context. Fried (1970) not only
discusses the idea of equality in relation to a Rawlsian
theory of justice, but also devotes a great deal of
space to problems relevant to philosophy and welfare,
for example, the concept of privacy in connection with
the probationary control of offenders.

Much of the literature in social administration barely
rises above a descriptive, institutional level. I have

found the most useful works to be those published by the
Centre for Studies in Social Policy under the editorship
of Rudolf Klein (1974;   1975), which are two volumes in
a continuing series.   Although ostensibly concerned with
the public expenditure aspects of social policy, they
review wider issues in the field, often taking unconven-
tional but persuasive stands on the topics they discuss.
In addition to this regular series, there is a large
amount of work in social administration detailing
inequalities in service provision.   An example of this
genre is provided by Bosanquet and Townsend (1972).
The basic trouble with this approach is that it tends
to regard service and income inequalities as instances of
political sin, only remediable by strength of socialist
will, rather than a result of a conflict of political
goals combined with the inevitable constraints on
public policy making.   Moreover, the description of
inequality is a statistical minefield, and the reader
is best advised to read such works in conjunction with
the contributions to be found in Beckerman (1972),
particularly the article by Michael Stewart, which
presents a more accurate picture.

Perhaps the most interesting piece of political
argument to emerge from the field of social administration is by Titmuss (1970).   Although primarily concerned
with the supply of blood for transfusion purposes,
Titmuss's work raises many more general issues in
connection with the role of altruism in social relations
and the moral attractiveness of market systems of
transfer in the social policy field.   It should, however,
be read in conjunction with Arrow (1971), who reveals
some inconsistencies in the argument and provides
evidence to suggest that some of Titmuss's empirical
assumptions are wrong or questionable.   Very little
work has been done by social administrators applying
the analytic methods used in the study of political
argument to problems of resource allocation and
priorities in the social welfare services.   However,
Judge (1976) provides an instance of what can be done,
in his examination of efficiency and rationing in the
personal social services.

Economists have been the other group professionally
to involve themselves with problems of social policy.
Both Collard (1972) and Culyer (1973) provide good
introductions to this approach from differing stand-
points.   Friedman (1962) provides a vigorous case for
an extension of the free market into areas of social
policy.   He also propounds the case for educational
vouchers, which can be best followed up by looking at

the literature cited in Maynard (1975).   For a number
of useful articles on the economic approach to health
services see Cooper and Culyer (1973).

Finally a word about journals.   There is no one
journal concerned with the subject of political argument
and social policy.   However, both the 'Journal of Social
Policy' and 'Philosophy and Public Affairs' publish
articles of relevance, and they are worth looking at
on a regular basis for this reason.   The best way of
filling the gap left by the absence of a regular
periodical is to keep up with the publications of the
'International Library of Welfare and Philosophy' series.

Bibliography

The following bibliography contains only works referred
to in the text, and is in no way intended to be a full
bibliography for works in political theory on the subject
of equality. A full entry is given for each item
referred to. Where more than one edition or version of
the work is available I give the date of the original
publication in the text and corresponding details in
the bibliography. Where I have used a version other
than the original, I give details after the original
entry, and this is the version to which the page numbers
in the text refer. For some writers (e.g., Aristotle)
it is obviously impossible to give an original publication date, so I have simply cited the name of the work
in the text and given the date of the edition used in
the bibliography.

ACTON, H.B. (1971), 'The Morals of Markets', Longman,
London.
ALLEN, R.G.D. (1962), 'Basic Mathematics', Macmillan,
London.
ANDERSON, O.W. (1972), 'Health Care: Can There Be Equity?
The United States, Sweden and England', Wiley, New York.
ARISTOTLE, (1962 edn), 'The Politics', trans T.A.
Sinclair, Penguin Books, Harmondsworth.
ARROW, K.J. (1963), 'Social Choice and Individual Values',
Yale University Press, New Haven.
ARROW, K.J. (1963b), Uncertainty and the Welfare Economics
of Medical Care, 'American Economic Review', vol. LIII, no.
5, pp. 941-73, reprinted in M.H. Cooper and A.J. Culyer
(eds), 'Health Economics', Penguin Books, Harmondsworth.
ARROW, K.J. (1971), Gifts and Exchanges, 'Philosophy
and Public Affairs', vol. 1, no. 4, pp. 343-62.
ATKINSON, A.B. (1969), 'Poverty in Britain and the Reform
of Social Security', Cambridge University Press.

BAGEHOT, W. (1867), 'The English Constitution', R.H.S. Crossman (ed.), Fontana, London.

BARNA, T. (1945),'Redistribution of Incomes Through Public Finance in 1937',Clarendon Press, Oxford.

BARNES, J. (1974), A Solution to Whose Problem?, in H. Glennerster and S. Hatch, 'Positive Discrimination and Inequality', pp. 9-13, Fabian Research Series 314, Fabian Society, London.

BARRY, B.M. (1965), 'Political Argument', Routledge & Kegan Paul, London.

BARRY, B.M. (1973), 'The Liberal Theory of Justice', Clarendon Press, Oxford.

BEARDSLEY, M.C. (1964), Equality and Obedience to Law, in 'Law and Philosophy', ed. S. Hook, pp. 35-42, New York University Press.

BECKERMAN, W. (ed.) (1972), Objectives and Performance: Overall View, in 'The Labour Government's Economic Record: 1964-1970', pp. 29-74, Duckworth, London.

BEDAU, H.A. (1967), Egalitarianism and the Idea of Equality, in 'Equality', Nomos IX, Pennock, J.R. and Chapman, J.W., pp. 3-27, Atherton Press, New York.

BELL, D. (1960), 'The End of Ideology', Free Press, Chicago, 1964.

BENN, S.I. and PETERS, R.S. (1959), 'Social Principles and the Democratic State', Allen & Unwin, London.

BERGSON, A. (1966), 'Essays in Normative Economics', Harvard University Press, Cambridge, Mass.

BERGSON, A. (1967), Market Socialism Revisited, in 'Journal of Political Economy', vol. 75, no. 5, pp. 655-73.

BERLIN, I. (1956), Equality, 'PAS', ns. vol. LVI, pp. 301-26.

BLACKSTONE, W.T. (1967), On the Meaning and Justification of the Equality Principle, in'Ethics', vol. 77, no. 4, pp. 239-53.

BOWIE, N.E. (1970), Equality and Distributive Justice, in 'Philosophy', vol. XLV, no. 172.

BOSANQUET, N. and TOWNSEND, P. (1972), 'Labour and Inequality', Fabian Society, London.

BRETON, A. (1974), 'The Economic Theory of Representative Government', Macmillan, London.

BRITTAN, S. (1968), 'Left or Right, The Bogus Dilemma', Secker & Warburg, London.

BRITTAN, S. (1969), 'Steering the Economy', Penguin Books, Harmondsworth.

BROWN, C.V. (1968), Misconceptions About Income Tax and Incentives in 'Scottish Journal of Political Economy', vol. 15, pp. 1-21.

BRUCE, M. (1961), 'The Coming of the Welfare State', Batsford, London.

BUCHANAN, J.J. (1965), 'The Inconsistencies of the
National Health Service', IEA Occasional Paper No. 7,
London.
BUTLER, D.E. and STOKES, D. (1974), 'Political Change
in Britain', second edition, Macmillan, London.
COLLARD, D. (1972), 'Prices, Markets and Welfare',
Faber & Faber, London.
COLEMAN, J.S. (1968), 'The Concept of Equality of
Educational Opportunity' in 'Harvard Educational Review',
vol. 38, no. 1, pp. 7-22.
COOPER, M.H. (1975), 'Rationing Health Care', Croom
Helm, London.
COOPER, M.H. and CULYER, A.J. (1972), Equality in the
National Health Service: Intentions, Performance and
Problems in Evaluation, M.M. Hauser: 'The Economics
of Medical Care', pp. 47-57, Penguin Books, Harmondsworth.
COOPER, M.H. and CULYER, A.J. (1973), 'Health Economics',
Penguin Books, Harmondsworth.
CULYER, A.J. (1973), 'Economics of Social Policy',
Martin Robertson, London.
CROSLAND, C.A.R. (1956), 'The Future of Socialism',
Jonathan Cape, London.
DAHL, R.A. (1961), 'Who Governs?', Yale University
Press, New Haven.
DASGUPTA, P. (1974), On Rawls' Conception of Distributive
Justice, 'Theory and Decision', vol. 4, no. 3/4, pp. 325-44.
DAVIES, B. (1968), 'Social Needs and Resources in Local
Services', Michael Joseph, London.
DANIELS, N. (1975), 'Reading Rawls', Blackwell, Oxford.
DOBB, M. (1969), 'Welfare Economics and the Economics
of Socialism', Cambridge University Press.
EMMET, D.M. (1969), Justice, in 'PAS', supp. vol. XLIII,
pp. 123-40.
FLATHMAN, R.E. (1967), Equality and Generalization, A
Formal Analysis, in 'Equality', J.R. Pennock and
J.W. Chapman (eds), pp. 38-60, Atherton Press, New York.
FRIED, C. (1970), 'An Anatomy of Values', Harvard
University Press, Cambridge, Mass.
FRIEDMAN, M. (1962), 'Capitalism and Freedom',
University of Chicago Press, 1963.
GALBRAITH, J.K. (1955), 'Economics and the Art of
Controversy', Rutgers University Press, New Brunswick N.J.
GEACH, P.T. (1960), Ascriptivism, in 'Philosophical
Review', vol. 69, pp. 221-5.
GLENNESTER, H. (1975), 'Social Service Budgets and
Social Policy', Allen & Unwin, London.
GODWIN, W. (1798), 'Enquiry Concerning Political Justice',
K. Codell Carter (ed.), Clarendon, Oxford, 1971.
GOLDTHORPE, J.H. (1974), Social Inequality and Social

Integration in Modern Britain, in D. Wedderburn (ed.),
'Poverty, Inequality and Class Structure', pp. 217-38,
Cambridge University Press.
GRAFF, J. de V. (1957), 'Theoretical Welfare Economics',
Cambridge University Press.
GRAHAM, A.C. (1965), Liberty and Equality in 'Mind',
vol. 74, no. 293, pp. 59-65.
GRAY, J. (1975), Positive Discrimination in Education:
A Review of the British Experience, in 'Policy and
Politics', vol. 4, no. 2, pp. 85-110.
HARE, R.M. (1952), 'The Language of Morals',
Clarendon Press, Oxford.
HARE, R.M. (1963), 'Freedom and Reason', Clarendon Press,
Oxford.
HARSANYI, J.C. (1955), Cardinal Welfare, Individualistic
Ethics, and Interpersonal Comparisons of Utility, in
'Journal of Political Economy', vol. 63, no. 4,
pp. 309-21. Reprinted in E.S. Phelps, 'Economic Justice',
pp. 266-85, Penguin Books, Harmondsworth.
HART, H.L.A. (1951), The Ascription of Responsibility
and Rights, in 'Logic and Language', A.G.N. Flew (ed.),
First Series, pp. 145-66, Blackwell, Oxford.
HART, H.L.A. (1955), Are There Any Natural Rights?, in
'Philosophical Review', vol. 64, pp. 175-91. Reprinted
in A. Quinton, 'Political Philosophy', pp. 53-66,
Oxford University Press.
HART, H.L.A. (1961), 'The Concept of Law', Clarendon
Press, Oxford.
HART, H.L.A. (1968), 'Punishment and Responsibility',
Oxford University Press, 1970.
HUME, D. (1751), An Enquiry Concerning the Principles
of Morals, T.H. Green and T.H. Grose (eds), in 'Essays
Moral, Practical and Literary', vol. 2, pp. 169-287,
Longman, London.
ILO (1972), 'The Cost of Social Security, 1964-1966',
Geneva.
JEFFREY, R.C. (1965), 'The Logic of Decision', McGraw-
Hill, New York.
JENCKS, C. et al. (1973), 'Inequality', Allen Lane,
The Penguin Press, London.
JUDGE, J.K. (1976), 'Rationing the Personal Social
Services', report prepared on behalf of the Personal
Social Services Council (unpublished).
KEYNES, J.M. (1940), How To Pay For The War, in 'The
Collected Writings of John Maynard Keynes', vol. IX,
pp. 367-439, Macmillan, London, 1972.
KLEIN, R. et al. (1974), 'Social Policy and Public
Expenditure', Centre for Studies in Social Policy,
London.

KLEIN, R. et al. (1975), 'Priorities and Inflation',
Centre for Studies in Social Policy, London.

LANSBURY, R. (1972), 'Swedish Social Democracy', Young
Fabian Pamphlet no. 29, Fabian Society, London.

LEVIN, H.M. (1968), The Failure of the Public Schools
and The Free Market Remedy, in 'The Urban Review',
vol. 3, pp. 32-7.

LEYDEN, W. von (1963), On Justifying Inequality, in
'Political Studies', vol. XI, no. 1, pp. 58-70.

LINDSAY, C.M. (1969), Medical Care and the Economics
of Sharing, 'Economics', ns, no. 144, pp. 351-62.
Reprinted in M.H. Cooper and A.J. Culyer, 'Health
Economics', Penguin Books, Harmondsworth.

LUCAS, J.R. (1965), Against Equality, in 'Philosophy',
Oct. 1965, vol. XL, no. 154, pp. 296-307.

LUCAS, J.R. (1966), 'The Principles of Politics',
Clarendon Press, Oxford.

LUCE, R.D. and RAIFFA, H. (1957), 'Games and Decisions',
Wiley, New York.

LYNES, T. (1971), Clawback, in 'Family Poverty', D. Bull
(ed.), pp. 118-33, Duckworth, London.

LYONS, D. (1965), 'Forms and Limits of Utilitarianism',
Clarendon Press, Oxford.

LYONS, D. (1975), 'Nature and Soundness of the Contract
Argument', in Daniels, pp. 141-67.

MARQUAND, D. (1969), The Dilemmas of 'Revisionist'
Social Democracy, in 'Dissent', November-December.

MARSHALL, T.H. (1950), 'Citizenship and Social Class',
Cambridge University Press.

MARX, K. (1875), Critique of the Gotha Programme, vol. II,
in 'Selected Works of K. Marx and F. Engels', Foreign
Languages Publishing House, Moscow, 1951.

MAYNARD, A. (1975), 'Experiment with Choice in
Education', IEA, London.

MEADE, J.E. (1964), 'Efficiency, Equality and the
Ownership of Property', Allen & Unwin, London.

MEADE, J.E. (1972), Poverty in the Welfare State, in
'Oxford Economic Papers', vol. 24, no. 3, pp. 283-326.

MEADE, J.E. (1975), 'The Intelligent Radical's Guide
to Economic Policy', Allen & Unwin, London.

MILLER, D. (1976), 'Social Justice', Clarendon Press,
Oxford.

MINOGUE, K. (1963), 'The Liberal Mind', Methuen, London.

MISHAN, E.J. (1969), 'The Costs of Economic Growth',
Penguin Books, Harmondsworth.

MORTIMORE, G.W. (1968), An Ideal of Equality, in
'Mind', vol. 77, no. 306, pp. 222-42.

MYRDAL, G. (1960), 'Beyond The Welfare State',
Duckworth, London.

NAGEL, T. (1973), Rawls on Justice, in 'Philosophical Review', vol. 82, pp. 220-34.

NATH, S.K. (1968), 'A Reappraisal of Welfare Economics', Routledge & Kegan Paul, London.

NETZER, R. (1967), Housing Taxation and Housing Policy, in A.A. Nevitt (ed.), 'The Economic Problems of Housing', pp. 123-36, Macmillan, London.

NICHOLSON, J.L. (1974), Distribution and Redistribution of Income in the UK, in 'Poverty, Inequality and Class Structure', D. Wedderburn (ed.), pp. 71-91, Cambridge University Press.

NOZICK, R. (1974), 'Anarchy, State and Utopia', Blackwell, Oxford.

OAKESHOTT, M. (1962), 'Rationalism in Politics', Methuen, London.

OWEN, D. (1975), Why the Health Service Must Be Rationed, 'Sunday Times', 12 October 1975.

PATTANAIK, P.K. (1968), Risk, Impersonality and the Social Welfare Function, in 'Journal of Political Economy', vol. 76, December. Reprinted in E.S. Phelps (ed.), 'Economic Justice', Penguin Books, Harmondsworth, 1973, pp. 298-318.

PECHMAN, J.A., AARON, H.J. and TAUSSIG, M.K. (1968), 'Social Security: Perspectives for Reform', The Brookings Institution, Washington.

PIGOU, A.C. (1920), 'The Economics of Welfare', Macmillan, London.

PITCHER, G. (1960), Hart on Action and Responsibility, in 'Philosophical Review', vol. 69, pp. 226-35.

RAPHAEL, D.D. (1964), Conservative and Prosthetic Justice, in 'Political Studies', vol. 12, pp. 149-62. Reprinted in A. de Crespigny and A. Wertheimer (eds), 'Contemporary Political Theory', pp. 177-91.

RAPHAEL, D.D. (1970), 'Problems of Political Philosophy', Macmillan, London.

RAWLS, J. (1962), Justice and Fairness, in 'Philosophy, Politics and Society', second series, P. Laslett and W.G. Runciman (eds), pp. 132-57, Blackwell, Oxford.

RAWLS, J. (1967), Distributive Justice, in 'Philosophy, Politics and Society', third series, P. Laslett and W.G. Runciman (eds), pp. 58-82, Blackwell, Oxford. Reprinted in 'Economic Justice', pp. 319-62, E.S. Phelps (ed.), Penguin Books, Harmondsworth.

RAWLS, J. (1972), 'A Theory of Justice', Clarendon Press, Oxford.

REIN, M. (1970), 'Social Policy', Random House, New York.

RESCHER, N. (1972), 'Welfare: The Social Issues in Philosophical Perspectives', University of Pittsburgh Press.

ROBBINS, L. (1932), 'An Essay on the Nature and
Significance of Economic Science', Macmillan, London,
1952.
ROTHENBERG, J. (1961), 'The Measurement of Social
Welfare', Prentice-Hall, Englewood Cliffs.
ROWLEY, C.K. and PEACOCK, A.T. (1975), 'Welfare Economics:
A Liberal Restatement', Martin Robertson, London.
RUNCIMAN, W.G. (1966), 'Relative Deprivation and Social
Justice', Routledge & Kegan Paul, London.
RUNCIMAN, W.G. (1967), 'Social' Equality, in 'Philosophical
Quarterly', vol. 17, reprinted in W. G. Runciman,
'Sociology in its Place', pp. 210-11, Cambridge University
Press, 1970.
SAMUELSON, P.A. (1958), An Exact Consumption-Loan
Model of Interest With or Without the Social Contrivance
of Money, 'Journal of Political Economy', vol. 66,
no. 6, pp. 467-82.
SAVILLE, J. (1957), The Welfare State: An Historical
Approach, in 'New Reasoner', no. 3, pp. 5-25.
SCHWARTZ, A; (1973), Moral Neutrality and Primary Goods,
in 'Ethics', vol. 83, pp. 294-307.
SEN, A.K. (1970), 'Collective Choice and Social Welfare',
Holden-Bay, Inc., San Francisco.
SEN, A.K. (1973), 'On Economic Inequality', Clarendon
Press, Oxford.
SIDGWICK, H. (1874), 'The Methods of Ethics', Macmillan,
London, seventh edn, 1904.
STEPHEN, L. (1896), Social Equality, in 'Social Rights
and Duties', vol. 1, pp. 175-220. Swan Sonnenschein,
London.
STRACHEY, J. (1952), Tasks and Achievement of British
Labour, in 'New Fabian Essays', R.H.S. Crossman (ed.),
pp. 181-215 (1970), Turnstile Press, London.
TAWNEY, R.H. (1921), 'The Acquisitive Society', G. Bell
& Sons, London, 1948.
THOMPSON, D. (1958), The Welfare State: Discussion,
in 'New Reasoner', vol. 4, pp. 125-30.
TITMUSS, R.M. (1963), 'Essays on the Welfare State',
Allen & Unwin, London.
TITMUSS, R.M. (1965), The Limits of the Welfare State,
in 'New Left Review', no. 27, pp. 28-37.
TITMUSS, R.M. (1970), 'The Gift Relationship',
Allen & Unwin, London.
TOBIN, J. (1970), On Limiting the Domain of Inequality,
in 'Journal of Law and Economics', vol. 13, no. 2,
pp. 263-77.
VAIZEY, J. (1975), 'Whatever Happened to Equality?',
BBC Publications, London.
VLASTOS, G. (1962), Justice and Equality, in 'Social

Justice', R.B. Brandt (ed.), pp. 31-72, Prentice-Hall,
Englewood Cliffs, N.J.
WEBER, M. (1948), Class, Status and Party, in 'From
Max Weber', trans. and edited H.H. Gerth and C. Wright
Mills. Routledge & Kegan Paul, London, 1961.
WEDDERBURN, D. (1965), Facts and Theories of the Welfare
State, in 'Socialist Register', pp. 127-46, Merlin Press,
London.
WEST, P.A. (1973), Allocation and Equity in the Public
Sector: The Hospital Revenue Allocation Formula, in
'Applied Economics', vol. 5, no. 3, pp. 153-66.
WILENSKY, H.L. (1975), 'The Welfare State and Equality',
University of California Press, Berkeley.
WILLIAMS, B. (1962), The Idea of Equality, in 'Philosophy,
Politics and Society', second series, P. Laslett and
W.G. Runciman (eds), pp. 110-31, Blackwell, Oxford.
WILLIAMS, B. (1973), 'Problems of the Self', Cambridge
University Press.
WYNN, M. (1970), 'Family Policy', Michael Joseph,
London.

OFFICIAL PUBLICATIONS

Central Advisory Council for Education (1967), 'Children
and their Primary Schools' (Plowden Report), two vols,
HMSO, London.
DHSS (1969), 'National Superannuation and Social
Insurance', HMSO, London (Cmnd 3883).
DHSS (1971), 'Strategy for Pensions', HMSO, London
(Cmnd 4755).
DHSS (1975), 'First Interim Report of the Resources
Allocation Working Party: Allocation to Regions in
1976-77', HMSO, London.
HALSEY, A.H. (1972), 'Educational Priority', HMSO, London.
'Proposals for a Tax-Credits System', HMSO, London, 1972
(Cmnd 5116).
'Public Expenditure to 1977-78', HMSO, London, 1973
(Cmnd 5519).
'Public Expenditure to 1978-79', HMSO, London, 1975
(Cmnd 5879).
'Public Expenditure to 1979-80', HMSO, London, 1976
(Cmnd 6393).

Abilities and natural endow-
    ments, 33, 34, 35, 85,
    86, 114-15; distinguished
    from benefits, 38-9, 78;
    moral arbitrariness of,
    35-7
Acton, H.B., 31, 108, 113,
    118, 134
Altruism, 43, 118-19
Anderson, O.W., 128
Aristotle, 1, 3, 18
Arrow, K.J., 85, 136
Atkinson, A.B., 23, 24

Barna, T., 124
Barnes, J., 95
Barry, B.M., 15, 23, 28, 47,
    67, 101, 134, 135
Beardsley, M.C., 125
Beckerman, W., 2, 136
Bedau, H.A., 15, 125
Bell, D., 124
Benevolence, principle of,
    32, 58, 82
Benn, S.I., 17, 125
Bergson, A., 105
Berlin, I., 15, 16, 125
Blackstone, W.T., 125
Bosanquet, N., 136
Bowie, N.E., 21, 125
Breton, A., 75
Brittan, S., 1, 55, 89, 116
Brown, C.V., 114

Bruce, M., 26
Buchanan, J.M., 87, 89
Butler, D., 124, 127

Castle, B., 128
Child allowances, 22-5
Child Poverty Action Group,
    23
Coleman, J.S., 91
Collard, D., 136
Collectivism, 6-7, 84
Consistency and impartiality,
    20-1; as principle of
    treatment, 19-22
Contract: inter-generational,
    64; and legal responsi-
    bility, 13; theory of
    justice, 30, 33-40, 44
Cooper, M.H., 59, 60, 89,
    137
Crosland, C.A.R., 124
Culyer, A.J., 59, 136, 137

Dahl, R.A., 132
Daniels, N., 135
Dasgupta, P., 47
Davies, B., 110
Deafeasibility: concept of,
    13; and trade-off of
    principles, 15
DHSS, 8, 62, 129
Difference Principle, 33,
    39, 40

Dobb, M., 115

Education: and primary
  goods, 49, 90-1; and
  social policy, 4, 90-7,
  100, 105; and vouchers,
  93-7, 100, 110
Educational priority areas,
  95-6
Efficiency: administrative,
  59-61; economic, 9,
  40-4, 105
Emmet, D.M., 16, 125
Envy, 39, 40
Equality: and 'burden of
  proof', 14-19; and
  collectivism, 6-7, 108-13;
  and justice, 3, 30-3, 72,
  84, 91; and legal
  justice, 18; and pensions,
  65; as rule of taxation,
  17; and social services,
  59, 104-7, 120-1; as
  source of political
  argument, 1
Equality, procedural, 3,
  11-13, 17, 19; and consistency, 19-22; and
  defeasibility, 13-17
Equality, substantive, 3,
  9, 17, 19; defined,
  37, 38; and economic
  welfare, 30-1, 37, 79,
  121; as end-state
  principle, 39, 45; and
  principle of need, 69-71,
  72, 79; and self-respect,
  39-40, 101
Equity: principle of, 3,
  22, 28-9, 101, 102; and
  child allowances, 22-5;
  and compulsory insurance,
  74; and housing
  subsidies, 25-8, 98-100;
  and income/leisure mix,
  47; and retirement
  pensions, 64
Expectations, 9, 62, 65

Fairness, principle of, 82
Flatham, R.E., 125
Freedom, 9, 75, 93, 94, 107,
  108-10
Fried, C., 72, 77, 81, 135
Friedman, M., 93, 117, 131,
  136
Full line supply, 75-6

Galbraith, J.K., 4
Geach, P., 125
Glennester, H., 8
Godwin, W., 43, 127
Graaff, J. de V., 31
Graham, A.C., 15
Gray, J., 92

Halsey, A.H., 92
Harsanyi, J.C., 31, 52, 135
Hart, H.L.A., 13, 14, 18,
  82, 125
Health care, 4, 84-90, 100,
  105; National Health
  Service, 8, 54, 55, 56,
  85-90, 102; and need,
  71-82; regional varia-
  tions, 59, 85, 86; and
  the retired, 66
Housing, 4, 111, 114; as
  primary good, 49, 97-8;
  and subsidies, 25-8,
  98-100
Howe, G., 123
Humanity, principle of, 31,
  32, 58

ILO, 109
Incentives, 9, 41-2, 105,
  113-14
Income: distribution, 104,
  106; maintenance, 4,
  105
Incrementalism, 8
Indicators, social,
  59
Individualism, 6

Institute for Economic
   Affairs, 124

Jencks, C., 92, 94, 95
Joseph, Sir Keith, 128
Judge, K., 126, 128, 136
Justice, and consent, 80,
   106-7, 111; contract
   theory of, 30, 33-40, 44,
   79, 86, 91, 101, 106,
   119-21; distributive, 5,
   30-3, 81-2, 103, 118;
   end-state theories, 32,
   39, 47, 49, 61, 107, 110,
   114; entitlement theory,
   32, 107; and equality,
   3, 30-3, 72, 84, 85, 91;
   natural, 18, 125; pure
   procedural, 73; Rawlsian
   theory, 58, 107; time-
   slice theory, 78-9

Keynes, J.M., 22, 126
Klein, R., 5, 88, 99, 111,
   135

Lange, O., 132
Lansbury, R., 109
Leisure, 47
Levin, H.M., 92
Leyden, W. von, 125
Lindsay, C.M., 86
Local Authorities, 99-100,
   110-13
Lucas, J.R., 125, 134
Lynes, T., 126
Lyons, D., 36, 130

Markets, 64, 85, 89, 94, 97,
   104-5, 113-18
Marquand, D., 133
Marshall, T.H., 119
Marx, K., 67
Maynard, A., 93, 137

Meade, J.E., 27, 117, 132
Miller, D., 135
Minogue, K., 67
Mishan, E.J., 123
Mortimore, G.W., 17, 19, 135

Nagel, T., 39
Nath, S.K., 75, 127
National Superannuation and
   Social Insurance, 62-6
Need: concept of, 67-9;
   and equality, 67, 69-71,
   85; and health care,
   71-82, 86; minimum
   levels of, 77, 120;
   principle of, 3, 48, 78,
   111
Negative Income Tax, 98
Netzer, R., 126
Nicholson, J.L., 124
Nozick, R., 32, 38, 39, 108,
   110, 131, 133, 134

Oakeshott, M., 8
Owen, D., 130

Paternalism, 9-10, 54-8,
   74, 100, 101
Pay-As-You-Go, principle
   for pensions, 64-6
Pechman, J.A., 66
Pensions policy, 61-6
Personal Social Services,
   4, 49, 57, 71, 111
Peters, R.S., 17, 125
Pitcher, G., 125
Plato, 18
Plowden Report, 92, 131
Primary goods: and distributive principles, 45-53,
   83, 106, 120; and
   education, 90-1; and
   health care, 74; and
   housing, 97-8; and
   need, 68; and pensions,
   62-5

Public interest, principle of, 15, 16

Raphael, D.D., 50, 135
Rawls, J., 3, 31, 33, 34, 35, 39, 40, 43, 46, 58, 68, 106, 107, 127, 128, 134
Rein, M., 124
Relative price effect, 116
Rescher, N., 108, 130, 134
Risk distribution of, 72-82
Robbins, L., 52
Rothenburg, J., 75, 130
Runciman, W.G., 127, 135

Samuelson, P.A., 64, 129
Saville, J., 124
Savings principle for pensions, 63
Schwartz, A., 50
Self-Respect, 39-40, 101, 120
Sen, A.K., 20, 43, 54, 127, 135
Sidgwick, H., 21, 44, 65, 126, 129
Social mix, 101-2
Social policy: and citizenship, 119-22; and growth, 5, 7; and market, 113-18; and political argument, 5; and public expenditure, 4, 9, 76, 116; and public opinion, 5, 76, 114-16; redistributive effects, 7, 56-7; and the state, 108-13, 118
Social rights, 120
Social security, 49, 61-2, 89
Stabilisation commission, 117

Strategy For Pensions, 62-6
Stephen, L., 125
Stewart, M., 136
Stokes, D., 124, 127
Strachey, J., 124

Tawney, R.H., 43
Taxation, 55, 66, 85, 86, 89, 99, 115
Thompson, D., 67
Titmuss, R.M., 22, 86, 119, 124, 136
Tobin, J., 98
Townsend, P., 136
Transport Subsidies, 50, 105

Utilitarianism, 33, 82
Utility, principle of, 19, 31, 35, 43, 103

Vaizey, J., 123
Vlastos, G., 69, 135
Vouchers, Educational, 93-7, 100, 110

Weber, M., 30
Welfare: absolute level of, 38; economic, 31, 37, 45, 83, 92, 104; general, 10, 31; individual welfare function, 47-8, 52, 57; and primary goods, 45-58; social welfare function, 75
West, P.A., 60
Wilensky, H.L., 7, 111, 112, 115, 133
Williams, B., 33, 53, 135
Wynn, M., 23

Routledge Social Science Series

Routledge & Kegan Paul   London, Henley and Boston

39 Store Street, London WC1E 7DD
Broadway House, Newtown Road, Henley-on-Thames,
Oxon RG9 1EN
9 Park Street, Boston, Mass. 02108

Contents

International Library of Sociology 3
General Sociology 3
Foreign Classics of Sociology 4
Social Structure 4
Sociology and Politics 5
Criminology 5
Social Psychology 6
Sociology of the Family 6
Social Services 7
Sociology of Education 8
Sociology of Culture 8
Sociology of Religion 9
Sociology of Art and Literature 9
Sociology of Knowledge 9
Urban Sociology 10
Rural Sociology 10
Sociology of Industry and Distribution 10
Anthropology 11
Sociology and Philosophy 12
International Library of Anthropology 12
International Library of Social Policy 13
International Library of Welfare and Philosophy 13
Primary Socialization, Language and Education 14
Reports of the Institute of Community Studies 14
Reports of the Institute for Social Studies in Medical Care 15
Medicine, Illness and Society 15
Monographs in Social Theory 15
Routledge Social Science Journals 16
Social and Psychological Aspects of Medical Practice 16

*Authors wishing to submit manuscripts for any series in
this catalogue should send them to the Social Science Editor,
Routledge & Kegan Paul Ltd, 39 Store Street,
London WC1E 7DD*

● *Books so marked are available in paperback*
All books are in Metric Demy 8vo format (216 × 138mm approx.)

International Library of Sociology

General Editor   John Rex

GENERAL SOCIOLOGY

Barnsley, J. H. The Social Reality of Ethics. *464 pp.*
Belshaw, Cyril. The Conditions of Social Performance. *An Exploratory Theory. 144 pp.*
Brown, Robert. Explanation in Social Science. *208 pp.*
● Rules and Laws in Sociology. *192 pp.*
Bruford, W. H. Chekhov and His Russia. *A Sociological Study. 244 pp.*
Cain, Maureen E. Society and the Policeman's Role. *326 pp.*
●**Fletcher, Colin.** Beneath the Surface. *An Account of Three Styles of Sociological Research. 221 pp.*
Gibson, Quentin. The Logic of Social Enquiry. *240 pp.*
Glucksmann, M. Structuralist Analysis in Contemporary Social Thought. *212 pp.*
Gurvitch, Georges. Sociology of Law. *Preface by Roscoe Pound. 264 pp.*
Hodge, H. A. Wilhelm Dilthey. *An Introduction. 184 pp.*
Homans, George C. Sentiments and Activities. *336 pp.*
Johnson, Harry M. Sociology: *a Systematic Introduction. Foreword by · Robert K. Merton. 710 pp.*
●**Keat, Russell,** and **Urry, John.** Social Theory as Science. *278 pp.*
Mannheim, Karl. Essays on Sociology and Social Psychology. *Edited by Paul Keckskemeti. With Editorial Note by Adolph Lowe. 344 pp.*
   Systematic Sociology: *An Introduction to the Study of Society. Edited by J. S. Erös and Professor W. A. C. Stewart. 220 pp.*
Martindale, Don. The Nature and Types of Sociological Theory. *292 pp.*
●**Maus, Heinz.** A Short History of Sociology. *234 pp.*
Mey, Harald. Field-Theory. *A Study of its Application in the Social Sciences. 352 pp.*
Myrdal, Gunnar. Value in Social Theory: *A Collection of Essays on Methodology. Edited by Paul Streeten. 332 pp.*
Ogburn, William F., and **Nimkoff, Meyer F.** A Handbook of Sociology. *Preface by Karl Mannheim. 656 pp. 46 figures. 35 tables.*
Parsons, Talcott, and **Smelser, Neil J.** Economy and Society: *A Study in the Integration of Economic and Social Theory. 362 pp.*
Podgórecki, Adam. Practical Social Sciences. *About 200 pp.*
●**Rex, John.** Key Problems of Sociological Theory. *220 pp.*
   Sociology and the Demystification of the Modern World. *282 pp.*
●**Rex, John** (Ed.) Approaches to Sociology. *Contributions by Peter Abell, Frank Bechhofer, Basil Bernstein, Ronald Fletcher, David Frisby, Miriam Glucksmann, Peter Lassman, Herminio Martins, John Rex, Roland Robertson, John Westergaard and Jock Young. 302 pp.*
Rigby, A. Alternative Realities. *352 pp.*
Roche, M. Phenomenology, Language and the Social Sciences. *374 pp.*

Sahay, A. Sociological Analysis. *220 pp.*

Simirenko, Alex (Ed.) Soviet Sociology. *Historical Antecedents and Current Appraisals. Introduction by Alex Simirenko. 376 pp.*

Strasser, Hermann. The Normative Structure of Sociology. *Conservative and Emancipatory Themes in Social Thought. About 340 pp.*

Urry, John. Reference Groups and the Theory of Revolution. *244 pp.*

Weinberg, E. Development of Sociology in the Soviet Union. *173 pp.*

FOREIGN CLASSICS OF SOCIOLOGY

●Durkheim, Emile. Suicide. *A Study in Sociology. Edited and with an Introduction by George Simpson. 404 pp.*

●Gerth, H. H., and Mills, C. Wright. From Max Weber: *Essays in Sociology. 502 pp.*

●Tönnies, Ferdinand. Community and Association. (*Gemeinschaft und Gesellschaft.*) *Translated and Supplemented by Charles P. Loomis. Foreword by Pitirim A. Sorokin. 334 pp.*

SOCIAL STRUCTURE

Andreski, Stanislav. Military Organization and Society. *Foreword by Professor A. R. Radcliffe-Brown. 226 pp. 1 folder.*

Carlton, Eric. Ideology and Social Order. *Preface by Professor Philip Abrahams. About 320 pp.*

Coontz, Sydney H. Population Theories and the Economic Interpretation. *202 pp.*

Coser, Lewis. The Functions of Social Conflict. *204 pp.*

Dickie-Clark, H. F. Marginal Situation: *A Sociological Study of a Coloured Group. 240 pp. 11 tables.*

Glaser, Barney, and Strauss, Anselm L. Status Passage. *A Formal Theory. 208 pp.*

Glass, D. V. (Ed.) Social Mobility in Britain. *Contributions by J. Berent, T. Bottomore, R. C. Chambers, J. Floud, D. V. Glass, J. R. Hall, H. T. Himmelweit, R. K. Kelsall, F. M. Martin, C. A. Moser, R. Mukherjee, and W. Ziegel. 420 pp.*

Johnstone, Frederick A. Class, Race and Gold. *A Study of Class Relations and Racial Discrimination in South Africa. 312 pp.*

Jones, Garth N. Planned Organizational Change: *An Exploratory Study Using an Empirical Approach. 268 pp.*

Kelsall, R. K. Higher Civil Servants in Britain: *From 1870 to the Present Day. 268 pp. 31 tables.*

König, René. The Community. *232 pp. Illustrated.*

●Lawton, Denis. Social Class, Language and Education. *192 pp.*

McLeish, John. The Theory of Social Change: *Four Views Considered. 128 pp.*

Marsh, David C. The Changing Social Structure of England and Wales, 1871-1961. *288 pp.*

Menzies, Ken. Talcott Parsons and the Social Image of Man. *About 208 pp.*

●**Mouzelis, Nicos.** Organization and Bureaucracy. *An Analysis of Modern Theories. 240 pp.*

Mulkay, M. J. Functionalism, Exchange and Theoretical Strategy. *272 pp.*

Ossowski, Stanislaw. Class Structure in the Social Consciousness. *210 pp.*

●**Podgórecki, Adam.** Law and Society. *302 pp.*

Renner, Karl. Institutions of Private Law and Their Social Functions. *Edited, with an Introduction and Notes, by O. Kahn-Freud. Translated by Agnes Schwarzschild. 316 pp.*

SOCIOLOGY AND POLITICS

Acton, T. A. Gypsy Politics and Social Change. *316 pp.*

Clegg, Stuart. Power, Rule and Domination. *A Critical and Empirical Understanding of Power in Sociological Theory and Organisational Life. About 300 pp.*

Hechter, Michael. Internal Colonialism. *The Celtic Fringe in British National Development, 1536–1966. 361 pp.*

Hertz, Frederick. Nationality in History and Politics: *A Psychology and Sociology of National Sentiment and Nationalism. 432 pp.*

Kornhauser, William. The Politics of Mass Society. *272 pp. 20 tables.*

●**Kroes, R.** Soldiers and Students. *A Study of Right- and Left-wing Students. 174 pp.*

Laidler, Harry W. History of Socialism. *Social-Economic Movements: An Historical and Comparative Survey of Socialism, Communism, Co-operation, Utopianism; and other Systems of Reform and Reconstruction. 992 pp.*

Lasswell, H. D. Analysis of Political Behaviour. *324 pp.*

Martin, David A. Pacifism: *an Historical and Sociological Study. 262 pp.*

Martin, Roderick. Sociology of Power. *About 272 pp.*

Myrdal, Gunnar. The Political Element in the Development of Economic Theory. *Translated from the German by Paul Streeten. 282 pp.*

Wilson, H. T. The American Ideology. *Science, Technology and Organization of Modes of Rationality. About 280 pp.*

Wootton, Graham. Workers, Unions and the State. *188 pp.*

CRIMINOLOGY

Ancel, Marc. Social Defence: *A Modern Approach to Criminal Problems. Foreword by Leon Radzinowicz. 240 pp.*

Cain, Maureen E. Society and the Policeman's Role. *326 pp.*

Cloward, Richard A., and Ohlin, Lloyd E. Delinquency and Opportunity: *A Theory of Delinquent Gangs. 248 pp.*

Downes, David M. The Delinquent Solution. *A Study in Subcultural Theory. 296 pp.*

Dunlop, A. B., and McCabe, S. Young Men in Detention Centres. *192 pp.*

Friedlander, Kate. The Psycho-Analytical Approach to Juvenile Delinquency: *Theory, Case Studies, Treatment. 320 pp.*

Glueck, Sheldon, and Eleanor. Family Environment and Delinquency. *With the statistical assistance of Rose W. Kneznek. 340 pp.*

Lopez-Rey, Manuel. Crime. *An Analytical Appraisal. 288 pp.*

Mannheim, Hermann. Comparative Criminology: *a Text Book. Two volumes. 442 pp. and 380 pp.*

Morris, Terence. The Criminal Area: *A Study in Social Ecology. Foreword by Hermann Mannheim. 232 pp. 25 tables. 4 maps.*

Rock, Paul. Making People Pay. *338 pp.*

●**Taylor, Ian, Walton, Paul,** and **Young, Jock.** The New Criminology. *For a Social Theory of Deviance. 325 pp.*

●**Taylor, Ian, Walton, Paul,** and **Young, Jock** (Eds). Critical Criminology. *268 pp.*

SOCIAL PSYCHOLOGY

Bagley, Christopher. The Social Psychology of the Epileptic Child. *320 pp.*

Barbu, Zevedei. Problems of Historical Psychology. *248 pp.*

Blackburn, Julian. Psychology and the Social Pattern. *184 pp.*

●**Brittan, Arthur.** Meanings and Situations. *224 pp.*

Carroll, J. Break-Out from the Crystal Palace. *200 pp.*

●**Fleming, C. M.** Adolescence: Its Social Psychology. *With an Introduction to recent findings from the fields of Anthropology, Physiology, Medicine, Psychometrics and Sociometry. 288 pp.*

● The Social Psychology of Education: *An Introduction and Guide to Its Study. 136 pp.*

●**Homans, George C.** The Human Group. *Foreword by Bernard DeVoto. Introduction by Robert K. Merton. 526 pp.*

● Social Behaviour: *its Elementary Forms. 416 pp.*

●**Klein, Josephine.** The Study of Groups. *226 pp. 31 figures. 5 tables.*

Linton, Ralph. The Cultural Background of Personality. *132 pp.*

●**Mayo, Elton.** The Social Problems of an Industrial Civilization. *With an appendix on the Political Problem. 180 pp.*

Ottaway, A. K. C. Learning Through Group Experience. *176 pp.*

Plummer, Ken. Sexual Stigma. *An Interactionist Account. 254 pp.*

●**Rose, Arnold M.** (Ed.) Human Behaviour and Social Processes: *an Interactionist Approach. Contributions by Arnold M. Rose, Ralph H. Turner, Anselm Strauss, Everett C. Hughes, E. Franklin Frazier, Howard S. Becker, et al. 696 pp.*

Smelser, Neil J. Theory of Collective Behaviour. *448 pp.*

Stephenson, Geoffrey M. The Development of Conscience. *128 pp.*

Young, Kimball. Handbook of Social Psychology. *658 pp. 16 figures. 10 tables.*

SOCIOLOGY OF THE FAMILY

Banks, J. A. Prosperity and Parenthood: *A Study of Family Planning among The Victorian Middle Classes. 262 pp.*

Bell, Colin R. Middle Class Families: *Social and Geographical Mobility. 224 pp.*

Burton, Lindy. Vulnerable Children. *272 pp.*

Gavron, Hannah. The Captive Wife: *Conflicts of Household Mothers. 190 pp.*

George, Victor, and **Wilding, Paul.** Motherless Families. *248 pp.*

Klein, Josephine. Samples from English Cultures.
  1. Three Preliminary Studies and Aspects of Adult Life in England. *447 pp.*
  2. Child-Rearing Practices and Index. *247 pp.*

Klein, Viola. The Feminine Character. *History of an Ideology. 244 pp.*

McWhinnie, Alexina M. Adopted Children. *How They Grow Up. 304 pp.*

● **Morgan, D. H. J.** Social Theory and the Family. *About 320 pp.*

● **Myrdal, Alva,** and **Klein, Viola.** Women's Two Roles: *Home and Work. 238 pp. 27 tables.*

Parsons, Talcott, and **Bales, Robert F.** Family: Socialization and Interaction Process. *In collaboration with James Olds, Morris Zelditch and Philip E. Slater. 456 pp. 50 figures and tables.*

SOCIAL SERVICES

Bastide, Roger. The Sociology of Mental Disorder. *Translated from the French by Jean McNeil. 260 pp.*

Carlebach, Julius. Caring For Children in Trouble. *266 pp.*

George, Victor. Foster Care. *Theory and Practice. 234 pp.*
  Social Security: *Beveridge and After. 258 pp.*

George, V., and **Wilding, P.** Motherless Families. *248 pp.*

● **Goetschius, George W.** Working with Community Groups. *256 pp.*

Goetschius, George W., and **Tash, Joan.** Working with Unattached Youth. *416 pp.*

Hall, M. P., and **Howes, I. V.** The Church in Social Work. *A Study of Moral Welfare Work undertaken by the Church of England. 320 pp.*

Heywood, Jean S. Children in Care: *the Development of the Service for the Deprived Child. 264 pp.*

Hoenig, J., and **Hamilton, Marian W.** The De-Segregation of the Mentally Ill. *284 pp.*

Jones, Kathleen. Mental Health and Social Policy, 1845-1959. *264 pp.*

King, Roy D., Raynes, Norma V., and **Tizard, Jack.** Patterns of Residential Care. *356 pp.*

Leigh, John. Young People and Leisure. *256 pp.*

● **Mays, John.** (Ed.) Penelope Hall's Social Services of England and Wales. *About 324 pp.*

Morris, Mary. Voluntary Work and the Welfare State. *300 pp.*

Nokes, P. L. The Professional Task in Welfare Practice. *152 pp.*

Timms, Noel. Psychiatric Social Work in Great Britain (1939-1962). *280 pp.*

● Social Casework: *Principles and Practice. 256 pp.*

Young, A. F. Social Services in British Industry. *272 pp.*

7

SOCIOLOGY OF EDUCATION

Banks, Olive. Parity and Prestige in English Secondary Education: a Study in Educational Sociology. *272 pp.*

Bentwich, Joseph. Education in Israel. *224 pp. 8 pp. plates.*

●**Blyth, W. A. L.** English Primary Education. *A Sociological Description.*
    1. Schools. *232 pp.*
    2. Background. *168 pp.*

Collier, K. G. The Social Purposes of Education: *Personal and Social Values in Education. 268 pp.*

Dale, R. R., and **Griffith, S.** Down Stream: *Failure in the Grammar School. 108 pp.*

Evans, K. M. Sociometry and Education. *158 pp.*

●**Ford, Julienne.** Social Class and the Comprehensive School. *192 pp.*

Foster, P. J. Education and Social Change in Ghana. *336 pp. 3 maps.*

Fraser, W. R. Education and Society in Modern France. *150 pp.*

Grace, Gerald R. Role Conflict and the Teacher. *150 pp.*

Hans, Nicholas. New Trends in Education in the Eighteenth Century. *278 pp. 19 tables.*

● Comparative Education: *A Study of Educational Factors and Traditions. 360 pp.*

●**Hargreaves, David.** Interpersonal Relations and Education. *432 pp.*

● Social Relations in a Secondary School. *240 pp.*

Holmes, Brian. Problems in Education. *A Comparative Approach. 336 pp.*

King, Ronald. Values and Involvement in a Grammar School. *164 pp.*

School Organization and Pupil Involvement. *A Study of Secondary Schools.*

●**Mannheim, Karl,** and **Stewart, W. A. C.** An Introduction to the Sociology of Education. *206 pp.*

Morris, Raymond N. The Sixth Form and College Entrance. *231 pp.*

●**Musgrove, F.** Youth and the Social Order. *176 pp.*

●**Ottaway, A. K. C.** Education and Society: An Introduction to the Sociology of Education. *With an Introduction by W. O. Lester Smith. 212 pp.*

Peers, Robert. Adult Education: *A Comparative Study. 398 pp.*

Pritchard, D. G. Education and the Handicapped: *1760 to 1960. 258 pp.*

Stratta, Erica. The Education of Borstal Boys. *A Study of their Educational Experiences prior to, and during, Borstal Training. 256 pp.*

Taylor, P. H., Reid, W. A., and **Holley, B. J.** The English Sixth Form. *A Case Study in Curriculum Research. 200 pp.*

SOCIOLOGY OF CULTURE

Eppel, E. M., and **M.** Adolescents and Morality: *A Study of some Moral Values and Dilemmas of Working Adolescents in the Context of a changing Climate of Opinion. Foreword by W. J. H. Sprott. 268 pp. 39 tables.*

●**Fromm, Erich.** The Fear of Freedom. *286 pp.*

● The Sane Society. *400 pp.*

Mannheim, Karl. Essays on the Sociology of Culture. *Edited by Ernst Mannheim in co-operation with Paul Kecskemeti. Editorial Note by Adolph Lowe. 280 pp.*
Weber, Alfred. Farewell to European History: *or The Conquest of Nihilism. Translated from the German by R. F. C. Hull. 224 pp.*

SOCIOLOGY OF RELIGION

Argyle, Michael and **Beit-Hallahmi, Benjamin.** The Social Psychology of Religion. *About 256 pp.*
Glasner, Peter E. The Sociology of Secularisation. *A Critique of a Concept. About 180 pp.*
Nelson, G. K. Spiritualism and Society. *313 pp.*
Stark, Werner. The Sociology of Religion. *A Study of Christendom.*
Volume I. *Established Religion. 248 pp.*
Volume II. *Sectarian Religion. 368 pp.*
Volume III. *The Universal Church. 464 pp.*
Volume IV. *Types of Religious Man. 352 pp.*
Volume V. *Types of Religious Culture. 464 pp.*
Turner, B. S. Weber and Islam. *216 pp.*
Watt, W. Montgomery. Islam and the Integration of Society. *320 pp.*

SOCIOLOGY OF ART AND LITERATURE

Jarvie, Ian C. Towards a Sociology of the Cinema. *A Comparative Essay on the Structure and Functioning of a Major Entertainment Industry. 405 pp.*
Rust, Frances S. Dance in Society. *An Analysis of the Relationships between the Social Dance and Society in England from the Middle Ages to the Present Day. 256 pp. 8 pp. of plates.*
Schücking, L. L. The Sociology of Literary Taste. *112 pp.*
Wolff, Janet. Hermeneutic Philosophy and the Sociology of Art. *150 pp.*

SOCIOLOGY OF KNOWLEDGE

Diesing, P. Patterns of Discovery in the Social Sciences. *262 pp.*
●**Douglas, J. D.** (Ed.) Understanding Everyday Life. *370 pp.*
●**Hamilton, P.** Knowledge and Social Structure. *174 pp.*
Jarvie, I. C. Concepts and Society. *232 pp.*
Mannheim, Karl. Essays on the Sociology of Knowledge. *Edited by Paul Kecskemeti. Editorial Note by Adolph Lowe. 353 pp.*
Remmling, Gunter W. The Sociology of Karl Mannheim. *With a Bibliographical Guide to the Sociology of Knowledge, Ideological Analysis, and Social Planning. 255 pp.*

Remmling, Gunter W. (Ed.) Towards the Sociology of Knowledge. *Origin and Development of a Sociological Thought Style. 463 pp.*
Stark, Werner. The Sociology of Knowledge: *An Essay in Aid of a Deeper Understanding of the History of Ideas. 384 pp.*

URBAN SOCIOLOGY

Ashworth, William. The Genesis of Modern British Town Planning: *A Study in Economic and Social History of the Nineteenth and Twentieth Centuries. 288 pp.*
Cullingworth, J. B. Housing Needs and Planning Policy: *A Restatement of the Problems of Housing Need and 'Overspill' in England and Wales. 232 pp. 44 tables. 8 maps.*
Dickinson, Robert E. City and Region: *A Geographical Interpretation 608 pp. 125 figures.*
The West European City: *A Geographical Interpretation. 600 pp. 129 maps. 29 plates.*
● The City Region in Western Europe. *320 pp. Maps.*
Humphreys, Alexander J. New Dubliners: *Urbanization and the Irish Family. Foreword by George C. Homans. 304 pp.*
Jackson, Brian. Working Class Community: *Some General Notions raised by a Series of Studies in Northern England. 192 pp.*
Jennings, Hilda. Societies in the Making: *a Study of Development and Redevelopment within a County Borough. Foreword by D. A. Clark. 286 pp.*
●**Mann, P. H.** An Approach to Urban Sociology. *240 pp.*
Morris, R. N., and **Mogey, J.** The Sociology of Housing. *Studies at Berinsfield. 232 pp. 4 pp. plates.*
Rosser, C., and **Harris, C.** The Family and Social Change. *A Study of Family and Kinship in a South Wales Town. 352 pp. 8 maps.*
●**Stacey, Margaret, Batsone, Eric, Bell, Colin,** and **Thurcott, Anne.** Power, Persistence and Change. *A Second Study of Banbury. 196 pp.*

RURAL SOCIOLOGY

Haswell, M. R. The Economics of Development in Village India. *120 pp.*
Littlejohn, James. Westrigg: *the Sociology of a Cheviot Parish. 172 pp. 5 figures.*
Mayer, Adrian C. Peasants in the Pacific. *A Study of Fiji Indian Rural Society. 248 pp. 20 plates.*
Williams, W. M. The Sociology of an English Village: *Gosforth. 272 pp. 12 figures. 13 tables.*

SOCIOLOGY OF INDUSTRY AND DISTRIBUTION

Anderson, Nels. Work and Leisure. *280 pp.*

● **Blau, Peter M.**, and **Scott, W. Richard.** Formal Organizations: *a Comparative approach. Introduction and Additional Bibliography by J. H. Smith. 326 pp.*

Dunkerley, David. The Foreman. *Aspects of Task and Structure. 192 pp.*

Eldridge, J. E. T. Industrial Disputes. *Essays in the Sociology of Industrial Relations. 288 pp.*

Hetzler, Stanley. Applied Measures for Promoting Technological Growth. *352 pp.*
  Technological Growth and Social Change. *Achieving Modernization. 269 pp.*

Holloweﬂ, Peter G. The Lorry Driver. *272 pp.*

● **Oxaal, I., Barnett, T.,** and **Booth, D.** (Eds). Beyond the Sociology of Development. *Economy and Society in Latin America and Africa. 295 pp.*

Smelser, Neil J. Social Change in the Industrial Revolution: *An Application of Theory to the Lancashire Cotton Industry, 1770–1840. 468 pp. 12 figures. 14 tables.*

ANTHROPOLOGY

Ammar, Hamed. Growing up in an Egyptian Village: *Silwa, Province of Aswan. 336 pp.*

Brandel-Syrier, Mia. Reeftown Elite. *A Study of Social Mobility in a Modern African Community on the Reef. 376 pp.*

Dickie-Clark, H. F. The Marginal Situation. *A Sociological Study of a Coloured Group. 236 pp.*

Dube, S. C. Indian Village. *Foreword by Morris Edward Opler. 276 pp. 4 plates.*
  India's Changing Villages: *Human Factors in Community Development. 260 pp. 8 plates. 1 map.*

Firth, Raymond. Malay Fishermen. *Their Peasant Economy. 420 pp. 17 pp. plates.*

Gulliver, P. H. Social Control in an African Society: a Study of the Arusha, Agricultural Masai of Northern Tanganyika. *320 pp. 8 plates. 10 figures.*
  Family Herds. *288 pp.*

Ishwaran, K. Tradition and Economy in Village India: *An Interactionist Approach.*
  Foreword by Conrad Arensburg. 176 pp.

Jarvie, Ian C. The Revolution in Anthropology. *268 pp.*

Little, Kenneth L. Mende of Sierra Leone. *308 pp. and folder.*
  Negroes in Britain. *With a New Introduction and Contemporary Study by Leonard Bloom. 320 pp.*

Lowie, Robert H. Social Organization. *494 pp.*

Mayer, A. C. Peasants in the Pacific. *A Study of Fiji Indian Rural Society. 248 pp.*

Meer, Fatima. Race and Suicide in South Africa. *325 pp.*

11

Smith, Raymond T. The Negro Family in British Guiana: *Family Structure and Social Status in the Villages. With a Foreword by Meyer Fortes. 314 pp. 8 plates. 1 figure. 4 maps.*
Smooha, Sammy. Israel: Pluralism and Conflict. *About 320 pp.*

SOCIOLOGY AND PHILOSOPHY

Barnsley, John H. The Social Reality of Ethics. *A Comparative Analysis of Moral Codes. 448 pp.*
Diesing, Paul. Patterns of Discovery in the Social Sciences. *362 pp.*
●**Douglas, Jack D.** (Ed.) Understanding Everyday Life. *Toward the Reconstruction of Sociological Knowledge. Contributions by Alan F. Blum. Aaron W. Cicourel, Norman K. Denzin, Jack D. Douglas, John Heeren, Peter McHugh, Peter K. Manning, Melvin Power, Matthew Speier, Roy Turner, D. Lawrence Wieder, Thomas P. Wilson and Don H. Zimmerman. 370 pp.*
Gorman, Robert A. The Dual Vision. *Alfred Schutz and the Myth of Phenomenological Social Science. About 300 pp.*
Jarvie, Ian C. Concepts and Society. *216 pp.*
●**Pelz, Werner.** The Scope of Understanding in Sociology. *Towards a more radical reorientation in the social humanistic sciences. 283 pp.*
Roche, Maurice. Phenomenology, Language and the Social Sciences. *371 pp.*
Sahay, Arun. Sociological Analysis. *212 pp.*
Sklair, Leslie. The Sociology of Progress. *320 pp.*
Slater, P. Origin and Significance of the Frankfurt School. *A Marxist Perspective. About 192 pp.*
Smart, Barry. Sociology, Phenomenology and Marxian Analysis. *A Critical Discussion of the Theory and Practice of a Science of Society. 220 pp.*

International Library of Anthropology

General Editor Adam Kuper

Ahmed, A. S. Millenium and Charisma Among Pathans. *A Critical Essay in Social Anthropology. 192 pp.*
Brown, Paula. The Chimbu. *A Study of Change in the New Guinea Highlands. 151 pp.*
Gudeman, Stephen. Relationships, Residence and the Individual. *A Rural Panamanian Community. 288 pp. 11 Plates, 5 Figures, 2 Maps, 10 Tables.*
Hamnett, Ian. Chieftainship and Legitimacy. *An Anthropological Study of Executive Law in Lesotho. 163 pp.*
Hanson, F. Allan. Meaning in Culture. *127 pp.*
Lloyd, P. C. Power and Independence. *Urban Africans' Perception of Social Inequality. 264 pp.*

Pettigrew, Joyce. Robber Noblemen. *A Study of the Political System of the Sikh Jats. 284 pp.*

Street, Brian V. The Savage in Literature. *Representations of 'Primitive' Society in English Fiction, 1858–1920. 207 pp.*

Van Den Berghe, Pierre L. Power and Privilege at an African University. *278 pp.*

International Library of Social Policy

General Editor Kathleen Jones

Bayley, M. Mental Handicap and Community Care. *426 pp.*

Bottoms, A. E., and **McClean, J. D.** Defendants in the Criminal Process. *284 pp.*

Butler, J. R. Family Doctors and Public Policy. *208 pp.*

Davies, Martin. Prisoners of Society. *Attitudes and Aftercare. 204 pp.*

Gittus, Elizabeth. Flats, Families and the Under-Fives. *285 pp.*

Holman, Robert. Trading in Children. *A Study of Private Fostering. 355 pp.*

Jones, Howard, and **Cornes, Paul.** Open Prisons. *About 248 pp.*

Jones, Kathleen. History of the Mental Health Service. *428 pp.*

Jones, Kathleen, with **Brown, John, Cunningham, W. J., Roberts, Julian,** and **Williams, Peter.** Opening the Door. *A Study of New Policies for the Mentally Handicapped. 278 pp.*

Karn, Valerie. Retiring to the Seaside. *About 280 pp. 2 maps. Numerous tables.*

Thomas, J. E. The English Prison Officer since 1850: *A Study in Conflict. 258 pp.*

Walton, R. G. Women in Social Work. *303 pp.*

Woodward, J. To Do the Sick No Harm. *A Study of the British Voluntary Hospital System to 1875. 221 pp.*

International Library of Welfare and Philosophy

General Editors Noel Timms and David Watson

● **Plant, Raymond.** Community and Ideology. *104 pp.*

● **McDermott, F. E.** (Ed.) Self-Determination in Social Work. *A Collection of Essays on Self-determination and Related Concepts by Philosophers and Social Work Theorists. Contributors: F. P. Biestek, S. Bernstein, A. Keith-Lucas, D. Sayer, H. H. Perelman, C. Whittington, R. F. Stalley, F. E. McDermott, I. Berlin, H. J. McCloskey, H. L. A. Hart, J. Wilson, A. I. Melden, S. I. Benn. 254 pp.*

Ragg, Nicholas M. People Not Cases. *A Philosophical Approach to Social Work. About 250 pp.*

● **Timms, Noel,** and **Watson, David** (Eds). Talking About Welfare. *Readings in Philosophy and Social Policy. Contributors: T. H. Marshall, R. B. Brandt, G. H. von Wright, K. Nielsen, M. Cranston, R. M. Titmuss, R. S. Downie, E. Telfer, D. Donnison, J. Benson, P. Leonard, A. Keith-Lucas, D. Walsh, I. T. Ramsey. 320 pp.*

Primary Socialization, Language and Education

General Editor Basil Bernstein

Adlam, Diana S., *with the assistance of Geoffrey Turner and Lesley Lineker.* Code in Context. *About 272 pp.*

Bernstein, Basil. Class, Codes and Control. *3 volumes.*
  1. *Theoretical Studies Towards a Sociology of Language. 254 pp.*
  2. *Applied Studies Towards a Sociology of Language. 377 pp.*
● 3. *Towards a Theory of Educatiomal Transmission. 167 pp.*

Brandis, W., and **Bernstein, B.** Selection and Control. *176 pp.*

Brandis, Walter, and **Henderson, Dorothy.** Social Class, Language and Communication. *288 pp.*

Cook-Gumperz, Jenny. Social Control and Socialization. *A Study of Class Differences in the Language of Maternal Control. 290 pp.*

● **Gahagan, D. M.,** and **G. A.** Talk Reform. *Exploration in Language for Infant School Children. 160 pp.*

Hawkins, P. R. Social Class, the Nominal Group and Verbal Strategies. *About 220 pp.*

Robinson, W. P., and **Rackstraw, Susan D. A.** A Question of Answers. *2 volumes. 192 pp. and 180 pp.*

Turner, Geoffrey J., and **Mohan, Bernard A.** A Linguistic Description and Computer Programme for Children's Speech. *208 pp.*

Reports of the Institute of Community Studies

● **Cartwright, Ann.** Parents and Family Planning Services. *306 pp.*
    Patients and their Doctors. *A Study of General Practice. 304 pp.*

Dench, Geoff. Maltese in London. *A Case-study in the Erosion of Ethnic Consciousness. 302 pp.*

● **Jackson, Brian.** Streaming: *an Education System in Miniature. 168 pp.*

Jackson, Brian, and **Marsden, Dennis.** Education and the Working Class: *Some General Themes raised by a Study of 88 Working-class Children in a Northern Industrial City. 268 pp. 2 folders.*

Marris, Peter. The Experience of Higher Education. *232 pp. 27 tables.*
    Loss and Change. *192 pp.*

Marris, Peter, and **Rein, Martin.** Dilemmas of Social Reform. *Poverty and Community Action in the United States. 256 pp.*

Marris, Peter, and Somerset, Anthony. African Businessmen. *A Study of Entrepreneurship and Development in Kenya. 256 pp.*

Mills, Richard. Young Outsiders: *a Study in Alternative Communities. 216 pp.*

Runciman, W. G. Relative Deprivation and Social Justice. *A Study of Attitudes to Social Inequality in Twentieth-Century England. 352 pp.*

Willmott, Peter. Adolescent Boys in East London. *230 pp.*

Willmott, Peter, and Young, Michael. Family and Class in a London Suburb. *202 pp. 47 tables.*

Young, Michael. Innovation and Research in Education. *192 pp.*

● Young, Michael, and McGeeney, Patrick. Learning Begins at Home. *A Study of a Junior School and its Parents. 128 pp.*

Young, Michael, and Willmott, Peter. Family and Kinship in East London. *Foreword by Richard M. Titmuss. 252 pp. 39 tables.*
The Symmetrical Family. *410 pp.*

Reports of the Institute for Social Studies in Medical Care

Cartwright, Ann, Hockey, Lisbeth, and Anderson, John L. Life Before Death. *310 pp.*

Dunnell, Karen, and Cartwright, Ann. Medicine Takers, Prescribers and Hoarders. *190 pp.*

Medicine, Illness and Society

General Editor W. M. Williams

Robinson, David. The Process of Becoming Ill. *142 pp.*

Stacey, Margaret, *et al.* Hospitals, Children and Their Families. *The Report of a Pilot Study. 202 pp.*

Stimson, G. V., and Webb, B. Going to See the Doctor. *The Consultation Process in General Practice. 155 pp.*

Monographs in Social Theory

General Editor Arthur Brittan

● Barnes, B. Scientific Knowledge and Sociological Theory. *192 pp.*
Bauman, Zygmunt. Culture as Praxis. *204 pp.*

● Dixon, Keith. Sociological Theory. *Pretence and Possibility. 142 pp.*
Meltzer, B. N., Petras, J. W., and Reynolds, L. T. Symbolic Interactionism. *Genesis, Varieties and Criticisms. 144 pp.*

● Smith, Anthony D. The Concept of Social Change. *A Critique of the Functionalist Theory of Social Change. 208 pp.*

Routledge Social Science Journals

The British Journal of Sociology. *Editor – Angus Stewart; Associate Editor – Leslie Sklair. Vol. 1, No. 1 – March 1950 and Quarterly. Roy. 8vo. All back issues available. An international journal publishing original papers in the field of sociology and related areas.*

Community Work. *Edited by David Jones and Marjorie Mayo. 1973. Published annually.*

Economy and Society. *Vol. 1, No. 1. February 1972 and Quarterly. Metric Roy. 8vo. A journal for all social scientists covering sociology, philosophy, anthropology, economics and history. All back numbers available.*

Religion. Journal of Religion and Religions. *Chairman of Editorial Board, Ninian Smart. Vol. 1, No. 1, Spring 1971. A journal with an inter-disciplinary approach to the study of the phenomena of religion. All back numbers available.*

Year Book of Social Policy in Britain, The. *Edited by Kathleen Jones. 1971. Published annually.*

Social and Psychological Aspects of Medical Practice

Editor Trevor Silverstone

Lader, Malcolm. Psychophysiology of Mental Illness. *280 pp.*

● **Silverstone, Trevor,** and **Turner, Paul.** Drug Treatment in Psychiatry. *232 pp.*

Printed in Great Britain by
Lowe & Brydone Printers Limited, Thetford, Norfolk